how to start a food truck business

Ever Wondered How to Launch a Profitable Food Truck?

Uncover the Secrets Here!

Starting a food truck business can be an exciting and rewarding endeavor, but it also requires a lot of planning and hard work. Whether you're a seasoned chef looking to branch out on your own, or a food enthusiast with a passion for cooking, owning a food truck can be a great way to turn your love of food into a profitable business. In this guide, we'll provide you with all the information you need to launch and run a successful food truck business. From developing your concept and menu, to securing funding and navigating the legal and regulatory requirements, we'll cover it all. You'll also learn about marketing and promotion, managing your staff, and food safety and sanitation. With this guide, you'll have the tools and knowledge to take your food truck business from an idea to a reality.

Copyright © 2024

Content

Introduction: The appeal of starting a food truck business and an overview of what to expect in the book

Starting a food truck business can be a unique and exciting way to turn your passion for food into a profitable venture. Food trucks have become increasingly popular in recent years, as more and more people are looking for convenient and delicious food options on the go. Whether you're a seasoned chef or a food enthusiast with a passion for cooking, owning a food truck can be a great way to start your own business and be your own boss.

The appeal of starting a food truck business is multifaceted. For one, it can be a cost-effective way to start a food business, as the overhead costs are often lower than those of a traditional brick-and-mortar restaurant. Additionally, a food truck allows for more flexibility in terms of location and menu offerings. Food trucks can be moved to different areas to reach new customers, and the menu can be easily modified to reflect changing trends and customer preferences.

Another appeal of starting a food truck business is the ability to create a unique and personal brand. Food trucks have a distinctive and quirky aesthetic that can easily be incorporated into the branding and marketing of the business. This allows for a more personal connection with customers and can help to build a loyal customer base.

In this guide, you will learn about all the aspects of starting and running a successful food truck business. From developing your concept and menu, to securing funding and navigating the legal and regulatory requirements, you will learn about all the steps necessary to launch your food truck business. We will also cover the different ways to market and promote your food truck, how to effectively manage your staff and ensure food safety and sanitation. We will also help you understand the importance of customer service and how to provide excellent customer service to attract and retain customers.

Additionally, we will cover the important aspects of food truck operations and logistics, such as how to choose and outfit the right vehicle and equipment for your food truck business, how to find the right location and obtain the necessary permits, how to obtain the necessary insurance to protect your food truck business, and how to use social media and create an online presence to promote your food truck business.

We will also discuss the importance of food cost management, and how to develop a profitable menu and manage food cost effectively, as well as how to design and brand your food truck to stand out in the market, and how to participate in food truck festivals and events to increase visibility and generate revenue.

Moreover, you will learn about the benefits of joining food truck associations and networks, how to maintain your vehicle and equipment to ensure safety and longevity, how to choose and implement mobile payment and point of sale systems for your food truck business, and how to manage accounting and bookkeeping for your food truck business.

We will also cover the importance of inventory management, and how to manage inventory and track food cost effectively, how to obtain the necessary licenses and certifications to operate your food truck business, how to accommodate customers with food allergies and special dietary needs, how to manage employee schedules and ensure adequate staffing and how to expand your business by offering catering services for events and parties.

Additionally, we will discuss how to expand your food truck business by opening additional trucks or franchising, and how to overcome common challenges that food truck business owners face, and how to grow and scale your food truck business for long-term success.

In summary, this guide will provide you with all the information you need to launch and run a successful food truck business. From developing your concept and menu, to securing funding and navigating the legal and regulatory requirements, you will have the tools and knowledge to take your food truck business from an idea to a reality. With this guide, you will be able to turn your passion for food into a profitable venture,

and enjoy the freedom and flexibility that comes with owning your own business.

It's important to note that starting a food truck business is not without its challenges. It can be difficult to navigate the legal and regulatory requirements, and securing funding can be a daunting task. Additionally, managing a food truck business requires a significant amount of time and effort, as well as a strong understanding of the industry.

However, with the right knowledge and preparation, starting a food truck business can be a rewarding and fulfilling experience. By understanding the various aspects of the food truck industry, you can make informed decisions and develop a strong business plan to ensure success.

In this guide, we will provide you with a comprehensive overview of the food truck industry, including market trends and current industry statistics. We will also provide you with practical advice and tips for starting and running a food truck business, including information on business planning, financing, legal and regulatory requirements, vehicle and equipment, operations and logistics, marketing and promotion, and customer service.

We will also provide you with information on food safety and sanitation, inventory management, accounting and bookkeeping, and how to handle food allergies and special dietary needs. Additionally, we will discuss the importance of participating in food truck festivals and events, as well as the benefits of joining food truck associations and networks.

Overall, this guide will provide you with the information you need to launch and run a successful food truck business. With the right preparation and understanding of the industry, you can turn your passion for food into a profitable venture and enjoy the freedom and flexibility that comes with owning your own business.

Concept Development: How to come up with a unique concept and menu for your food truck business

Concept development is one of the most important steps in starting a food truck business. A unique and well-defined concept can help to differentiate your business from competitors and attract customers. It also helps to guide menu development, marketing and promotion, and overall operations.

When developing your concept, it's important to consider your target market, as well as your own personal strengths and interests. For example, if you have a passion for a particular type of cuisine or cooking style, that can be a great starting point for your concept. Similarly, if you know that there is a demand for a particular type of food in your area, that can be a good opportunity to capitalize on.

It's also important to consider how your concept will fit into the current food truck scene in your area. Researching existing food truck businesses in your area can give you an idea of what concepts are already popular and what gaps there may be in the market. Additionally, you can also look into food trends to see what types of food are currently popular.

Once you have a general idea of your concept, it's important to fine-tune and define it further. This includes creating a mission statement for your business, which should reflect your concept and your overall goals for the business. It's also important to consider how your concept will be communicated to customers through branding and marketing.

When developing your menu, it's important to consider how it fits into your overall concept and target market. A well-designed menu should not only feature dishes that align with your concept, but also be reflective of your target market's tastes and preferences. Additionally, it's important to consider food cost and profitability when developing your menu, as well as any food allergies or dietary restrictions that you may need to accommodate.

One way to come up with a unique concept and menu is to look into fusion cuisine, which is the combination of two or more different cuisines, this could be a great way to stand out in the market and offer customers something new and different. Another way to stand out is to focus on a particular dietary restriction, for example, vegan or gluten-free options, as this can attract a specific customer base that may be underserved in your area.

Additionally, it is important to keep in mind the feasibility of your menu items with the equipment and facilities that you have or plan to have on your food truck. Some items may require specific equipment or take up too much space, which can impact your operations and efficiency.

Another way to create a unique concept and menu is to focus on a specific cultural or regional cuisine that is underrepresented in your area. This can include ethnic cuisines like Korean or Peruvian, or regional specialties like Cajun or Tex-Mex. By focusing on a specific type of cuisine, you can differentiate your business and attract customers who are looking for something new and different.

It's also important to consider how you will source your ingredients. Using locally sourced and sustainable ingredients can not only support the local community but also can be a great way to differentiate your business and attract customers who are looking for high-quality, ethically-sourced food.

In summary, concept development is an essential step in starting a food truck business. By considering your target market, personal strengths, and current food trends, you can develop a unique and well-defined concept that can help to differentiate your business and attract customers. Additionally, by focusing on a specific cuisine or dietary restriction, sourcing ingredients locally and sustainably, and keeping in mind the feasibility of menu items with the equipment and facilities you have, you can create a menu that aligns with your concept and appeals to your target market.

Concept development is a crucial step in starting a food truck business, as it lays the foundation for the overall direction and success of the business. In addition to developing a unique and well-defined concept, it's important to also research the competition and market trends to ensure that your concept is feasible and has potential for success.

One important aspect of concept development is to identify your target market. This includes understanding their demographics, preferences, and purchasing habits. For example, if you plan to operate in a busy downtown area, your target market may be young professionals who are looking for quick, convenient, and delicious food options during their lunch break. On the other hand, if you plan to operate in a residential area, your target market may be families who are looking for affordable and easy dinner options. Understanding your target market can help you to create a concept and menu that appeals to them.

Another important aspect of concept development is to create a unique and compelling concept that differentiates your food truck from competitors. This can be achieved by focusing on a specific cuisine or cooking style, or by offering a unique and innovative menu that can't be found elsewhere. For example, you could focus on a specific regional cuisine that is underrepresented in your area, such as a Cajun or Tex-Mex food truck, or you could offer a unique fusion cuisine that combines two or more different cuisines.

Additionally, you can also stand out by providing a specific dietary options such as vegan or gluten-free, this can attract customers who are looking for specific food options. You can also differentiate your business by sourcing your ingredients locally and sustainably, and by incorporating eco-friendly and sustainable practices into your operations.

Researching the competition and market trends can also provide valuable insights into what concepts are already popular in your area and what gaps there may be in the market. This can help you to identify opportunities and make informed decisions about your concept and menu. For example, if you notice that there are already several food trucks in your area that offer burgers, you may want to consider a different concept that would appeal to customers looking for something different, such as a food truck that specializes in seafood.

It's also important to keep in mind the feasibility of your concept and menu with the equipment and facilities you have or plan to have on your food truck. Some items may require specific equipment or take up too much space, which can impact your operations and efficiency.

In summary, concept development is a crucial step in starting a food truck business that lays the foundation for the overall direction and success of the business. By identifying your target market, creating a unique and compelling concept, researching the competition and market trends, and keeping in mind the feasibility of your concept and menu with your equipment and facilities, you can develop a concept that has the potential for success and attract customers.

Concept development is a crucial step in starting a food truck business and it is an ongoing process that should be continuously evaluated and refined as the business grows. One way to come up with a unique concept and menu is to conduct customer research by surveys, focus groups or interviews to understand what customers are looking for in a food truck and what they think is missing from the current food truck scene in your area.

Another way to come up with a unique concept and menu is to experiment with different ingredients, cooking techniques, and flavors to create a distinct and memorable menu. This can include incorporating global flavors, using unusual ingredients, or experimenting with different cooking methods. It's also important to keep in mind that your menu should be adaptable to different seasons and events. For example, you could offer seasonal items or special menus for holidays or sporting events.

In addition to creating a unique concept, it's also important to ensure that it's feasible and profitable. This includes understanding the costs associated with ingredients, equipment, and labor, as well as the potential revenue and profit margins. It's also important to conduct a break-even analysis to understand the point at which the business will start generating a profit.

Furthermore, it's important to keep in mind that your concept should be consistent and reflected in every aspect of your business. This includes your branding, marketing, customer service, and overall operations. Your concept should be easily recognizable to customers and should be communicated clearly and consistently through all of your business' touchpoints.

In conclusion, concept development is an ongoing and essential process for any food truck business. It's important to conduct research, experiment, and continuously evaluate and refine your concept

to ensure that it is unique, feasible, and profitable. By conducting customer research, experimenting with different ingredients and flavors, and being mindful of costs and profitability, you can create a concept and menu that stands out in the market and appeals to your target customers. Additionally, it's important to ensure that your concept is consistent across all aspects of your business and communicated clearly to customers.

One way to keep your concept fresh and engaging is to regularly update and experiment with your menu. This can include rotating seasonal items, introducing new dishes, or offering special menus for holidays or events. This can also help to attract repeat customers who are looking for something new and exciting.

Another way to keep your concept fresh and engaging is to actively engage with your customers. You can do this by soliciting feedback and suggestions for menu items, hosting customer events, and building a community around your food truck. This can help to create a loyal customer base and increase the visibility of your business.

It's also important to stay current with industry trends and adapt to changes in the market. This includes keeping an eye on food trends, new technologies, and changes in consumer preferences. By staying current, you can ensure that your concept and menu remain relevant and appealing to customers.

In summary, concept development is an ongoing process that requires research, experimentation, and adaptation. By being mindful of customer preferences, staying current with industry trends, and actively engaging with customers, you can create a concept and menu that stands out in the market and appeals to your target customers. Additionally, by regularly updating and experimenting with your menu, you can attract repeat customers and build a loyal customer base.

Business Planning: How to create a business plan and determine your target market

Creating a comprehensive business plan is an essential step in starting a food truck business. A business plan is a detailed document that outlines your business's goals, strategies, and financial projections. It serves as a roadmap for the development and growth of your business, and it is often required when seeking funding from investors or loans from banks.

When creating a business plan, it's important to include the following key elements:

Executive Summary: This section provides a brief overview of your business, including your concept, target market, and financial projections.

Industry Analysis: This section provides an overview of the food truck industry, including market size, trends, and competition. It should also include information on the target market and customer demographics.

Business Description: This section provides a detailed description of your business, including your concept, mission statement, and overall goals. It should also include information on your management team, ownership structure, and any partnerships or collaborations.

Market Analysis: This section provides a detailed analysis of your target market, including customer demographics, purchasing habits, and market size. It should also include information on your competition and market trends.

Sales and Marketing: This section outlines your sales and marketing strategies, including how you plan to promote your business and attract customers. It should also include information on pricing, promotions, and advertising.

Operations and Logistics: This section provides a detailed description of your operations and logistics, including information on your food truck, equipment, and facilities. It should also include information on your supply chain, inventory management, and food safety.

__Financial Projections: This section provides financial projections for your business, including projected income statements, balance sheets, and cash flow statements. It should also include information on funding requirements and projected return on investment.__

Determining your target market is a critical step in creating a business plan and in developing your overall business strategy. Your target market is the group of customers that your business will focus on, and it is important to understand their demographics, purchasing habits, and preferences in order to create a concept and menu that appeals to them.

To determine your target market, you should first conduct market research to gather information about the food truck industry, the competition, and the local market in your area. This research can be done by conducting surveys, focus groups, or interviews with potential customers. Additionally, you can also gather information from industry reports, government statistics, and

other sources.

Once you have gathered information about the industry and market, you can then begin to identify your target market. This includes understanding their demographics, such as age, gender, income, education, and occupation. Additionally, you should also consider their purchasing habits and preferences, such as what types of food they like, how often they eat out, and where they typically purchase their food.

It's also important to consider the location of your food truck and how it will impact your target market. For example, if you plan to operate in a busy downtown area, your target market may be young professionals who are looking for quick, convenient, and delicious food options during their lunch break. On the other hand, if you plan to operate in a residential area, your target market may be families who are looking for affordable and easy dinner options.

Once you have identified your target market, you can then create a concept and menu that appeals to them. For example, if your target market is young professionals, you may want to focus on offering healthy and convenient meal options. On the other hand, if your target market is families, you may want to focus on offering affordable and kid-friendly options.

It's also important to note that your target market may change over time, and you should be prepared to adapt your concept and menu accordingly. For example, as the food truck industry evolves, new trends and consumer preferences may emerge, and you may need to adapt your concept and menu to stay competitive.

In summary, creating a comprehensive business plan is an essential step in starting a food truck business. It serves as a roadmap for the development and growth of your business, and it is often required when seeking funding from investors or loans from banks. Determining your target market is a critical step in creating a business plan and in developing your overall business strategy. By conducting market research, identifying your target market, and creating a concept and menu that appeals to them, you can create a business plan that has the potential for success and attract customers. Additionally, it's important to be prepared to adapt your target market and concept as the industry and consumer preferences evolve over time.

Financing: How to secure funding for your food truck business and manage your finances

Securing financing is an essential step in starting a food truck business. The costs associated with purchasing or leasing a food truck, as well as purchasing equipment, inventory, and other expenses, can be significant. As a result, many food truck owners turn to various forms of financing to help fund their business.

There are several options available for financing a food truck business, including:

Small Business Administration (SBA) Loans: The SBA offers a variety of loan programs that can help small businesses, including food truck businesses, secure financing. These loans are often easier to obtain than traditional bank loans, and they often have lower interest rates and more flexible terms.

Bank Loans: Banks offer a variety of loan options for small businesses, including food truck businesses. These loans can be used for the purchase of equipment, inventory, and other expenses. Banks may also offer lines of credit, which can provide a source of working capital for your business.

Crowdfunding: Crowdfunding allows individuals to invest small amounts of money in a business venture in exchange for rewards or equity. This can be a good option for food truck businesses that are looking for smaller amounts of funding and are willing to offer rewards or equity in return.

Angel Investors: Angel investors are individuals who provide financing in exchange for equity in a business. These investors can be a good option for food truck businesses that are looking for larger amounts of funding and are willing to give up a percentage of ownership in return.

Personal Savings: Personal savings is one of the most common ways to finance a food truck business. If you have sufficient savings, you may be able to fund your business entirely on your own.

It's important to remember that whichever financing option you choose, it's important to have a solid business plan in place. A business plan can help you to secure funding by providing detailed information about your business, including your concept, target market, and financial projections.

Managing your finances is an important aspect of running a food truck business. It's important to keep accurate financial records, including income and expenses, to ensure that

your business is profitable. This includes creating a budget, tracking your expenses, and monitoring your cash flow.

Creating a budget is an essential step in managing your finances. A budget will help you to determine how much money you need to cover your expenses and how much you need to bring in to make a profit. It should include fixed costs, such as the cost of the food truck, equipment, and inventory, as well as variable costs, such as the cost of ingredients and labor. By creating a budget, you can identify areas where you may need to cut costs or increase revenue in order to improve your bottom line.

It's also important to track your expenses to ensure that you are staying within your budget. This includes keeping accurate records of all of your expenses, including the cost of ingredients, equipment, and labor. By tracking your expenses, you can identify areas where you may be overspending and make adjustments accordingly.

Monitoring your cash flow is also an important aspect of managing your finances. Cash flow is the amount of money coming in and going out of your business. By monitoring your cash flow, you can ensure that you have enough money to cover your expenses and make a profit. This includes tracking your income, including sales, as well as your expenses, including the cost of ingredients, equipment, and labor.

Managing your finances also involves protecting yourself against financial risks. This includes obtaining the necessary insurance for your business, such as liability insurance, to protect yourself against potential lawsuits. It also includes managing your taxes, including keeping accurate records of your income and expenses, and ensuring that you are in compliance with state and federal tax laws.

Another important aspect of managing your finances is to maintain a good credit score. This can be achieved by paying bills on time, keeping your debt levels low, and maintaining a good credit history. A good credit score can help you to secure financing for your business, and it can also help you to obtain better terms on loans and other forms of financing.

Finally, it's important to seek the advice of a financial advisor or accountant. They can help you to create a budget, monitor your cash flow, and make informed financial decisions for your business. They can also help you to navigate the complex legal and tax requirements of running a business, which can help you to avoid potential financial pitfalls.

In summary, securing financing and managing your finances are essential steps in starting a food truck business. There are several options available for financing a food truck business, including SBA loans, bank loans, crowdfunding, angel investors, and personal savings. Managing your finances includes creating a budget, tracking your expenses, monitoring your cash flow, protecting yourself against financial risks, maintaining a good credit score, and seeking the advice of a financial advisor or accountant. By managing your finances effectively, you can ensure that your business is profitable and has the resources to grow and succeed in the long term.

Legal and Regulatory Requirements: How to navigate the legal and regulatory requirements of starting a food truck business

Navigating the legal and regulatory requirements of starting a food truck business can be a complex and time-consuming process. It's important to understand and comply with all of the laws and regulations that apply to your business in order to operate legally and avoid potential fines and penalties.

Here are some of the key legal and regulatory requirements that food truck businesses need to be aware of:

Business Licensing: Depending on your location, you may need to obtain a business license, food service permit, or mobile food vending permit in order to operate your food truck. These licenses and permits are typically issued by the local health department or city government and may require passing an inspection and meeting certain health and safety standards.

Food Safety: Food truck businesses are subject to the same food safety laws and regulations as restaurants and other food service establishments. This includes compliance with food handling and storage requirements, sanitation standards, and food safety training for employees. It's important to ensure that your food truck is equipped with proper food storage, cooking, and cleaning equipment, and that your employees are trained in safe food handling practices.

Zoning and Parking: Food truck businesses are also subject to zoning and parking laws and regulations. This includes obtaining permission to operate in certain areas, such as city parks or downtown districts, and ensuring that your food truck is parked in designated areas.

Insurance: It's important to have insurance to protect your business and customers from potential accidents, injuries, or liability. This includes liability insurance, vehicle insurance, and worker's compensation insurance.

Taxation: Food truck businesses are subject to the same tax laws and regulations as other small businesses. This includes registering for a sales tax permit, collecting and remitting sales tax, and filing business income taxes. It's important to keep accurate records of your income and expenses to ensure compliance with tax laws and to minimize your tax liability.

Employee regulations: As an employer, you are responsible for following laws and regulations regarding the hiring, management, and payment of employees. This includes compliance with minimum wage laws, overtime laws

, and laws related to employee benefits, such as healthcare and retirement plans. It's also important to ensure that your hiring practices are in compliance with anti-discrimination laws and to have a clear and compliant employee handbook that outlines policies and procedures.

Intellectual property: It's also important to protect your business's intellectual property such as name, logo, and branding. This includes registering trademarks and copyrights, and ensuring that your branding and marketing materials do not infringe on the intellectual property rights of others.

Environmental regulations: Food truck businesses may also be subject to environmental regulations, such as proper disposal of waste and adherence to emissions standards.

It's important to note that laws and regulations can vary by location, and it's essential to research and comply with the specific laws and regulations that apply to your business. Furthermore, it's important to stay up-to-date with any changes or updates to these laws and regulations as they can change over time.

In conclusion, navigating the legal and regulatory requirements of starting a food truck business can be complex and time-consuming, but it's essential to ensure that your business is operating legally and protecting your customers and employees. This includes obtaining the necessary licenses and permits, complying with food safety regulations, following zoning and parking laws, obtaining insurance, and complying with tax laws and regulations. Additionally, it's important to research and comply with laws and regulations specific to your location and to stay up-to-date with any changes or updates to these laws. Seeking the advice of legal or professional advisers is also important in order to ensure that your business is in compliance with all the laws and regulations.

Vehicle and Equipment: How to choose and outfit the right vehicle and equipment for your food truck business

Choosing and outfitting the right vehicle and equipment for your food truck business is an important step in ensuring the success of your business. The right vehicle and equipment can make the difference between a smooth and efficient operation and a chaotic and unreliable one.

Here are some key factors to consider when choosing and outfitting your food truck:

Vehicle: The type of vehicle you choose will depend on the size and scale of your operation, as well as your budget. Common options include vans, trailers, and buses, but it's important to choose a vehicle that is in good condition and that meets all safety and health regulations. It's also important to consider factors such as fuel efficiency, maintenance costs, and maneuverability.

Equipment: The equipment you choose will depend on the type of food you plan to serve, as well as the size and scale of your operation. Common equipment includes a commercial kitchen, a refrigerator, a grill or stove, and a sink. It's important to choose equipment that is durable, easy to maintain, and energy-efficient. It's also important to ensure that the equipment you choose meets all safety and health regulations.

Power source: A reliable power source is essential for operating your food truck. This can include a generator, solar panels, or a hookup to an external power source. It's important to choose a power source that is reliable and that can provide enough power to run all of your equipment.

Ventilation and air conditioning: Proper ventilation and air conditioning are important for the health and safety of your customers and employees, as well as the quality of your food. It's important to choose a ventilation and air conditioning system that is effective and that meets all safety and health regulations.

Storage: Adequate storage is essential for keeping your food and supplies fresh and organized. It's important to choose a storage system that is efficient and that maximizes the use of space.

Signage and branding: Visibility and branding are important for attracting customers to your food truck. It's important to choose signs and branding that are visible, eye-catching, and that clearly communicate your business's name, menu and contact information.

It's important to note that laws and regulations regarding vehicles and equipment can vary by location, and it's essential to research and comply with the specific laws and regulations that apply to your business. Additionally, it's important to consider the cost and maintenance of the vehicle and equipment, as well as its potential resale value.

In conclusion, choosing and outfitting the right vehicle and equipment for your food truck business is essential for the

success and efficiency of your business. Factors to consider include the size and scale of your operation, your budget, and the type of food you plan to serve. It's important to choose a vehicle that is in good condition, meets all safety and health regulations, and is fuel-efficient and easy to maneuver. Additionally, it's important to choose equipment that is durable, easy to maintain, energy-efficient, and meets all safety and health regulations. A reliable power source, proper ventilation and air conditioning, adequate storage, and effective signage and branding are also key considerations. It's important to comply with the specific laws and regulations that apply to your business, and to consider the cost and maintenance of the vehicle and equipment, as well as its potential resale value. Seeking the advice of industry professionals is also a good idea to ensure that you make the best choices for your business.

Operations and Logistics: How to plan for and execute the daily operations and logistics of your food truck business

Operations and logistics are critical components of running a successful food truck business. They involve the planning and execution of the day-to-day tasks that are necessary to keep your business running smoothly. From sourcing ingredients and managing inventory, to setting up at events and serving customers, effective operations and logistics are essential for the success of your business.

Here are some key aspects of operations and logistics to consider when *starting a food truck business:*

Menu planning: Developing a menu that appeals to your target market and is profitable is essential. This includes considering the cost of ingredients, the time and skill required to prepare each item, and the prices you will charge for each item. It's also important to have a plan for rotating menu items and for dealing with food waste.

Sourcing ingredients: Sourcing ingredients that are high-quality, affordable, and consistent is important for maintaining the quality of your food and keeping costs under control. This includes developing relationships with suppliers, and understanding the different options available for sourcing ingredients, such as purchasing from local farms, or from large commercial suppliers.

Inventory management: Effective inventory management is essential for ensuring that you have the ingredients and supplies you need to operate your food truck, while keeping costs under control. This includes keeping accurate records of what you have on hand, what you need to purchase, and when. It also includes developing a system for ordering and receiving supplies and for storing and rotating ingredients to ensure they are fresh.

Preparing food: Preparing food on a food truck can be challenging, as space and resources are limited. It's important to have a plan for preparing food in advance, as well as for keeping food at the right temperature and for dealing with food waste.

Setting up and serving customers: Setting up and serving customers on a food truck can be challenging, as space and resources are limited. It's important to have a plan for setting up in different locations, for dealing with weather and other environmental factors, and for dealing with customer complaints.

Staffing: Staffing is a critical component of running a food truck business, and it's important to have a plan for hiring, training, and managing employees. This includes developing a schedule, assigning duties, and dealing with employee complaints.

Marketing: Marketing is an important aspect of a food truck business, as it's what draws customers to your business. This includes developing a marketing plan, creating a website, and using social media to promote your business.

Maintenance: Regular maintenance is important for ensuring that your food truck and equipment are in good condition and are able to operate efficiently. This includes scheduling regular maintenance and repairs, and keeping accurate records of when maintenance was performed.

Safety and sanitation: Safety and sanitation are critical components of running a food truck business, and it's important to have a plan for maintaining a clean and safe environment. This includes complying with all health and safety regulations, and developing procedures for dealing

with potential hazards and emergencies.

Logistics: Logistics is the process of planning and executing the movement of goods and people. In the context of a food truck business, logistics includes planning the schedule and route of the food truck, coordinating with events and locations, and dealing with any issues that may arise during transportation.

Technology: Technology can play a significant role in operations and logistics, from inventory management software to GPS tracking and mobile payment systems. It's important to have a plan for incorporating technology into your business, and to stay up to date with the latest tools and systems available.

Scalability: As your food truck business grows, it's important to have a plan for scaling up your operations and logistics. This includes expanding your menu, hiring more staff, and investing in larger or additional vehicles and equipment.

In conclusion, operations and logistics are critical components of running a successful food truck business. Effective menu planning, sourcing ingredients, inventory management, preparing food, setting up and serving customers, staffing, marketing, maintenance, safety and sanitation, logistics, technology, and scalability are all important aspects to consider. It's important to have a plan for each of these areas and to continually evaluate and improve your processes as your business evolves. It's also important to stay up-to-date with laws and regulations and to seek the advice of industry professionals when necessary. With a solid plan in place, your food truck business will be well-positioned to operate efficiently and successfully.

Marketing and Promotion: How to effectively market and promote your food truck business

Marketing and promotion are critical components of any business, and a food truck business is no exception. Effective marketing and promotion can help to attract customers, increase sales, and grow your business. However, marketing and promotion for a food truck business can be challenging, as the business is mobile and the target market may be different from a traditional brick-and-mortar restaurant. Here are some key strategies for effectively marketing and promoting your food truck business:

Develop a strong brand: Your brand is the overall image and reputation of your business. It's important to develop a strong brand that reflects your business's values and mission, and that differentiates your business from competitors. This includes developing a logo, colors, and a consistent message that is used across all of your marketing materials.

Create a website and social media presence: A website and social media presence are essential for reaching potential customers. Your website should be user-friendly and provide information about your business, including your menu, location, and hours of operation. Social media platforms, such as Facebook, Instagram, and Twitter, are an effective way to engage with customers, promote your business, and build a community around your brand.

Use traditional marketing methods: Traditional marketing methods, such as flyers, brochures, and billboards, can be effective for reaching potential customers. It's important to choose marketing methods that are appropriate for your target market and that are cost-effective.

Participate in community events: Participating in community events, such as festivals and fairs, can help to build awareness of your business and attract new customers. It's important to choose events that are appropriate for your target market and that have a large attendance.

Partner with other businesses: Partnering with other businesses, such as local shops or other food trucks, can help to expand your reach and promote your business. Partnerships can include collaborations on events, social media campaigns, or cross-promotions.

Offer discounts and promotions: Offering discounts and promotions can be an effective way to attract customers and increase sales. This can include offering discounts to repeat customers, or promoting a new menu item.

Use customer reviews and testimonials: Positive customer reviews and testimonials can be an effective way to promote your business. Encourage customers to leave reviews on your website and social media platforms, and use these reviews in your marketing materials.

Utilize Food-Delivery apps: Utilizing food-delivery apps such as UberEats, Grub

Hub and DoorDash can help to increase your visibility and reach potential customers who may not have known about your food truck otherwise. This can also help to increase sales and revenue, as customers can order and pay through the app, and have the food delivered to their location.

Leverage Influencer Marketing: Leveraging influencer marketing can be an effective way to reach a large audience and promote your business. Identify influencers in your industry or local area who have a large following on social media, and work with them to create sponsored content or host an event at your food truck.

Use Analytics: Utilizing analytics tools such as Google Analytics or Facebook Insights can help you to track the performance of your marketing campaigns and understand your target audience better. This can help you to make data-driven decisions about where to focus your marketing efforts, and how to improve the ROI of your campaigns.

In conclusion, marketing and promotion are critical components of a successful food truck business. It's important to develop a strong brand, create a website and social media presence, use traditional marketing methods, participate in community events, partner with other businesses, offer discounts and promotions, use customer reviews and testimonials, utilize food-delivery apps, leverage influencer marketing and use analytics to track the performance of your campaigns. It's also important to stay up-to-date with the latest trends and technology in marketing and to continually evaluate and improve your marketing strategies. With a solid marketing plan in place, your food truck business will be well-positioned to attract customers, increase sales, and grow your business.

Managing a mobile business, such as a food truck, comes with unique challenges that are not present in traditional brick-and-mortar businesses. These challenges include navigating the logistics and operations of a mobile business, dealing with the limitations of a mobile kitchen, and adapting to the constantly changing environment. However, with the right planning and strategies in place, these challenges can be overcome and a mobile business can be run successfully.

Navigating logistics and operations: Operating a food truck requires a great deal of planning and coordination. This includes scheduling events and locations, coordinating with other food trucks and vendors, and dealing with the logistics of setting up and breaking down the truck at each location. It's important to have a system in place for managing these logistics, such as a schedule and route planner, and to have a clear plan for dealing with any unexpected issues that may arise.

Dealing with limitations of a mobile kitchen: A food truck is a mobile kitchen and therefore, space and resources are limited. This can make it difficult to prepare and serve food, and it's important to have a plan for dealing with these limitations. This includes investing in equipment that is designed for a mobile kitchen, such as compact and portable appliances, and having a plan for food preparation and storage.

Adapting to a constantly changing environment: A food truck operates in a constantly changing environment, and it's important to be adaptable and flexible. This includes dealing with weather and other environmental factors, adapting to different locations and events, and being able to adjust to changes in customer demand and preferences.

Maintaining a strong online presence: A strong online presence is essential for reaching potential customers and promoting your business. This includes having a website, being active on social media, and using online tools such as food-delivery apps to increase visibility and reach a larger audience.

Building relationships with other vendors and businesses: Building relationships with other vendors and businesses in your industry can be beneficial for your mobile business. This includes networking with other food truck owners, partnering with other businesses for events, and collaborating on marketing and promotional campaigns.

Managing finances: Managing finances is critical for the success of any business, but it can be especially challenging for a mobile business. This includes tracking income and expenses, keeping accurate records, and developing a budget that allows for the unique costs of operating a mobile business.

Developing a strong brand: Developing a strong brand that reflects the values and mission of your business is essential for building a loyal customer base. This includes creating a memorable logo, consistent messaging, and a unique selling proposition that differentiates your business from competitors.

Implementing safety and sanitation measures: Safety and sanitation are critical to the success of a food truck business, and it's important to have a plan in place for maintaining a clean and safe environment. This includes complying with all health and safety regulations, and developing procedures for dealing with potential hazards and emergencies.

Staying up-to-date with regulations and laws: Staying up-to-date with regulations and laws is essential for operating a legal and compliant mobile business. This includes obtaining the necessary licenses and permits, complying with health and safety regulations, and understanding the laws and regulations that pertain to mobile businesses in your area.

Continuously evaluating and improving: Running a mobile business requires constant evaluation and adaptation. It's important to continuously evaluate your operations and logistics, marketing and *promotion strategies, and financials, and make changes as necessary. This includes gathering feedback from customers, tracking your progress and performance, and seeking out new opportunities for growth and expansion.*

In conclusion, managing a mobile business, such as a food truck, comes with unique challenges. However, with the right planning and strategies in place, these challenges can be overcome. Navigating logistics and operations, dealing with the limitations of a mobile kitchen, adapting to a constantly changing environment, maintaining a strong online presence, building relationships with other vendors and businesses, managing finances, developing a strong brand, implementing safety and sanitation measures, staying up-to-date with regulations and laws, and continuously evaluating and improving are all critical components of running a successful mobile business. With a strong plan in place, your food truck business can navigate the unique challenges of operating a mobile business and operate efficiently and successfully.

Managing Your Staff: How to effectively manage your staff and create a positive work culture

Managing your staff is a critical component of running a successful food truck business. A positive work culture and effective management techniques can lead to increased productivity, improved employee morale, and lower turnover rates. Here are some key strategies for managing your staff and creating a positive work culture:

Hire the right people: Hiring the right people is essential for creating a positive work culture. This includes identifying the skills and qualifications that are required for each position, as well as the personality traits and work ethic that will be a good fit for your business. It's also important to conduct thorough interviews and reference checks, and to provide new hires with a thorough orientation and training program.

Communicate effectively: Communication is a key component of effective management, and it's important to establish clear and open lines of communication between management and staff. This includes holding regular meetings, providing regular updates and feedback, and being available to answer questions and address concerns.

Set clear expectations: Setting clear expectations for employees is essential for creating a positive work culture. This includes outlining job responsibilities, setting performance goals and standards, and providing regular feedback and evaluations.

Foster a positive work environment: Fostering a positive work environment is essential for creating a positive work culture. This includes providing a safe and clean working environment, promoting teamwork, and recognizing and rewarding good performance.

Provide opportunities for growth: Providing opportunities for growth is essential for creating a positive work culture. This includes providing training and development programs, promoting from within, and encouraging employees to take on new challenges and responsibilities.

Encourage employee engagement: Encouraging employee engagement is essential for creating a positive work culture. This includes providing opportunities for employees to give feedback, recognizing and rewarding good performance, and promoting a sense of ownership and accountability.

Develop a strong team: Developing a strong team is essential for creating a positive work culture. This includes promoting teamwork, fostering a sense of camaraderie, and encouraging employees to support one another.

Lead by example: Leading by example is essential for creating a positive work culture. This includes setting a good example in terms of work ethic, attitude, and behavior, and being approachable and supportive.

Be adaptable and flexible: Being adaptable and flexible is essential for managing a mobile business. This includes being open to change and new ideas, and being willing to make adjustments as necessary.

Continuously evaluate and improve: Continuously evaluating and improving your management strategies is essential for creating a positive work culture. This includes gathering feedback from employees, tracking performance, and making adjustments as necessary.

In conclusion, managing your staff and creating a positive work culture is critical for the success of a food truck

business. Hiring the right people, communicating effectively, setting clear expectations, fostering a positive work environment, providing opportunities for growth, encouraging employee engagement, developing a strong team, leading by example, being adaptable and flexible, and continuously evaluating and improving are all key strategies for managing your staff effectively. It's important to understand the unique challenges of managing a mobile business and to create a management strategy that is tailored to the needs of your business. Additionally, it's important to stay up-to-date with laws and regulations related to labor, and to seek the advice of industry professionals when necessary. With a strong management strategy in place, your food truck business will be well-positioned to create a positive work culture, increase productivity, improve employee morale, and lower turnover rates.

Food Safety and Sanitation: How to ensure food safety and sanitation in your food truck business

Food safety and sanitation are critical components of running a successful food truck business. Ensuring food safety and sanitation can help to prevent foodborne illnesses, protect the reputation of your business, and comply with regulations and laws. Here are some key strategies for ensuring food safety and sanitation in your food truck business:

Follow food safety guidelines: Following food safety guidelines is essential for ensuring food safety and sanitation. This includes adhering to the food safety guidelines set forth by the FDA, as well as any additional guidelines that may be specific to your state or local area. This also includes adhering to the guidelines for food storage, preparation, and handling.

Train your staff on food safety: Training your staff on food safety is essential for ensuring food safety and sanitation. This includes providing regular training on food safety guidelines, as well as ongoing training on new food safety techniques and procedures.

Maintain a clean and sanitary environment: Maintaining a clean and sanitary environment is essential for ensuring food safety and sanitation. This includes regularly cleaning and sanitizing the food truck, as well as the equipment and utensils used in food preparation.

Properly store and label food: Properly storing and labeling food is essential for ensuring food safety and sanitation. This includes storing food at the appropriate temperature, as well as labeling food with the date it was prepared and the date it should be consumed by.

Practice good personal hygiene: Practicing good personal hygiene is essential for ensuring food safety and sanitation. This includes regularly washing hands, wearing gloves when handling food, and keeping hair tied back and covered.

Regularly check and maintain equipment: Regularly checking and maintaining equipment is essential for ensuring food safety and sanitation. This includes checking and cleaning equipment, such as refrigeration units, on a regular basis, and ensuring that equipment is in good working condition.

Have a plan in place for dealing with foodborne illnesses: Having a plan in place for dealing with foodborne illnesses is essential for ensuring food safety and sanitation. This includes having procedures in place for dealing with foodborne illnesses, such as reporting incidents to the appropriate authorities, and having a plan in place for preventing future incidents.

Regularly check and comply with regulations and laws: Regularly checking and complying with regulations and laws is essential for ensuring food safety and sanitation. This includes staying up-to-date with food safety regulations and laws, and ensuring that the food truck is in compliance with all relevant regulations and laws.

Use food thermometer: Using a food thermometer is essential for ensuring food safety and sanitation. This includes using a thermometer to check the temperature of food, and ensuring that food is cooked to the appropriate temperature before serving.

Build a relationship with a local health department: Building a

relationship with a local health department is essential for ensuring food safety and sanitation. This includes regularly communicating with the health department, participating in health inspections, and seeking out guidance and advice on food safety and sanitation best practices.

In conclusion, food safety and sanitation are critical components of running a successful food truck business. Following food safety guidelines, training your staff on food safety, maintaining a clean and sanitary environment, properly storing and labeling food, practicing good personal hygiene, regularly checking and maintaining equipment, having a plan in place for dealing with foodborne illnesses, regularly checking and complying with regulations and laws, using food thermometer, and building a relationship with a local health department are all key strategies for ensuring food safety and sanitation. It's important to understand the unique challenges of operating a mobile kitchen, and to create a food safety and sanitation plan that is tailored to the needs of your business. By implementing these strategies, your food truck business will be well-positioned to ensure food safety and sanitation, prevent foodborne illnesses, protect the reputation of your business, and comply with regulations and laws.

Overcoming Challenges: How to overcome common challenges that food truck business owners face

Running a food truck business comes with its own set of challenges, but with the right strategies in place, these challenges can be overcome. Here are some common challenges that food truck business owners face, and how to overcome them:

Weather and location dependence: Food truck businesses rely heavily on weather and location, and inclement weather or a poor location can greatly impact sales. To overcome this challenge, it's important to have a plan in place for dealing with bad weather, such as offering indoor seating or delivery options, and to regularly evaluate and change locations to ensure maximum visibility and foot traffic.

Limited kitchen space and equipment: Food trucks have limited kitchen space and equipment, which can make it difficult to prepare and serve food. To overcome this challenge, it's important to invest in compact and portable equipment that is designed for a mobile kitchen, and to have a plan for food preparation and storage.

High operating costs: Operating a food truck can be costly, with expenses such as fuel, insurance, and maintenance. To overcome this challenge, it's important to have a budget in place and to regularly evaluate expenses to ensure that the business is operating efficiently.

Limited storage space: Food trucks have limited storage space for inventory and supplies, which can make it difficult to keep up with demand. To overcome this challenge, it's important to have a plan for inventory management and to regularly restock supplies.

Competition: Food trucks face competition from other food trucks, as well as traditional brick-and-mortar restaurants. To overcome this challenge, it's important to have a unique concept and menu, to differentiate your business from competitors, and to regularly evaluate and improve your marketing strategies.

Regulatory compliance: Food trucks are subject to various regulations and laws, such as health and safety codes, and it's important to stay up-to-date with these regulations and comply with them. To overcome this challenge, it's important to have a plan in place for complying with regulations and to regularly check and update the food truck's compliance status.

Staffing and management: Managing a staff and maintaining a positive work culture can be challenging for food truck business owners. To overcome this challenge, it's important to have a clear and effective management strategy in place, to hire the right people, and to provide regular training and opportunities for growth.

Marketing and promotion: Food trucks face challenges in reaching and attracting customers. To overcome this challenge, it's important to have a strong online presence, participate in community events, partner with other businesses, and use traditional marketing methods.

Financing: Securing funding for a food truck business can be difficult, and it's important to have a plan in place for managing

finances and securing funding. To overcome this challenge, it's important to create a detailed business plan and financial projections, to research and apply for funding options such as loans and grants, and to implement cost-saving measures and strategies for generating revenue.

Adapting to change: The food industry is constantly evolving, and food truck businesses need to be able to adapt to changing trends and consumer preferences. To overcome this challenge, it's important to stay informed about industry trends, to gather feedback from customers, and to be open to new ideas and approaches.

In conclusion, running a food truck business comes with its own set of challenges, but with the right strategies in place, these challenges can be overcome. Weather and location dependence, limited kitchen space and equipment, high operating costs, limited storage space, competition, regulatory compliance, staffing and management, marketing and promotion, financing, and adapting to change are all common challenges that food truck business owners face. By understanding these challenges and developing effective strategies for overcoming them, your food truck business will be well-positioned to navigate the unique challenges of operating a mobile business and operate efficiently and successfully.

Parking and permitting: Finding suitable parking and obtaining the necessary permits to operate in different areas can be a challenge for food truck businesses. To overcome this challenge, it's important to research parking and permitting regulations in different areas, to develop relationships with property owners and other businesses to secure parking spots, and to always have a backup plan in case a parking spot is unavailable.

Building a loyal customer base: Building a loyal customer base can be challenging for food truck businesses, especially for new businesses. To overcome this challenge, it's important to offer a unique and high-quality food experience, to engage with customers through social media and other marketing channels, and to offer loyalty programs and rewards to encourage repeat business.

Maintaining consistency in food quality and service: Maintaining consistency in food quality and service can be challenging in a mobile food business. To overcome this challenge, it's important to have detailed recipes and procedures in place, to provide regular training to the staff, and to regularly check and evaluate the food and service quality to ensure consistency.

Keeping up with Technology: Keeping up with technology and using it to improve the business can be a challenge for food truck business owners. To overcome this challenge, it's important to regularly research new technologies and tools that can help with operations, marketing, and customer engagement, and to invest in tools that will benefit the business.

Dealing with unexpected breakdowns: Dealing with unexpected breakdowns in equipment or vehicle can be a challenge for food truck businesses. To overcome this challenge, it's important to invest in high-quality equipment and vehicles, to regularly maintain and service them, and to have a plan in place for dealing with unexpected breakdowns such as having backup equipment or a backup vehicle.

Being able to offer a variety of menu options: Being able to offer a variety of menu options can be a challenge for food truck businesses due to the limited kitchen space and equipment. To overcome this challenge, it's important to focus on offering a limited menu that can be prepared quickly and efficiently, and to periodically change or rotate menu items to keep things fresh.

Managing inventory and keeping track of expenses: Managing inventory and keeping track of expenses can be challenging for food truck businesses. To overcome this challenge, it's important to have a system in place for inventory management, to regularly check and evaluate expenses, and to have a detailed budget in place to keep the business on track.

Building a strong online presence: Building a strong online presence can be challenging for food truck businesses. To overcome this challenge, it's important to have a website, social media accounts, and an active presence on food truck directories and review sites to attract customers and increase visibility.

In conclusion, owning and running a food truck business comes with its own set of challenges, but with the right strategies in place, these challenges can be overcome. Parking and permitting, building a loyal customer base, maintaining consistency in food quality and service, keeping up with technology, dealing with unexpected breakdowns, being able to offer a variety of menu options, managing inventory and keeping track of expenses, building a strong online presence, and many other challenges are all common challenges that food truck business owners face. By understanding these challenges and developing effective strategies for overcoming them, your food truck business will be well-positioned to navigate the unique challenges of operating a mobile business and operate efficiently and successfully.

Scaling and Growth: How to grow and scale your food truck business for long-term success

Scaling and growing a food truck business for long-term success requires careful planning and execution. Here are some strategies for scaling and growing your food truck business:

Develop a solid business plan: A solid business plan is essential for scaling and growing your food truck business. This includes creating a detailed plan for growth, outlining your target market, and identifying your unique value proposition.

Expand your customer base: To scale and grow your food truck business, you need to expand your customer base. This includes identifying new target markets and developing strategies for reaching and engaging with them.

Increase your offerings: Increasing your offerings is a great way to scale and grow your food truck business. This includes adding new menu items, offering catering services, and developing new revenue streams.

Invest in technology: Technology can be a powerful tool for scaling and growing your food truck business. This includes investing in point-of-sale systems, mobile ordering systems, and customer relationship management tools.

Optimize your operations: Optimizing your operations is essential for scaling and growing your food truck business. This includes streamlining your processes, automating tasks, and reducing costs.

Build a strong brand: Building a strong brand is essential for scaling and growing your food truck business. This includes developing a unique and consistent brand identity, developing a strong online presence, and creating a loyal customer base.

Foster a positive work culture: Foster a positive work culture is essential for scaling and growing your food truck business. This includes creating a supportive and collaborative work environment, recognizing employee contributions, and providing opportunities for growth and development.

Get involved in your community: Getting involved in your community is a great way to scale and grow your food truck business. This includes participating in community events, supporting local charities, and building relationships with other businesses.

Seek out partnerships and collaborations: Seeking out partnerships and collaborations is a great way to scale and grow your food truck business. This includes developing strategic partnerships with other businesses, collaborating with other food truck operators, and working with local organizations.

Continuously evaluate and improve: Continuously evaluating and improving is essential for scaling and growing your food truck business. This includes regularly assessing your business performance, gathering feedback from customers, and making changes and adjustments as needed.

In conclusion, scaling and growing a food truck business for long-term success requires careful planning and execution. Developing a solid business plan, expanding your customer base, increasing your offerings, investing in technology, optimizing your operations, building a strong brand, fostering a positive work culture, getting involved in your community, seeking out partnerships and collaborations, and continuously evaluating and improving are all strategies that can help you to scale and grow your food truck business for long-term success. It's important to have a clear vision for growth, and to develop a plan that is tailored to the needs of your business and your target market. By implementing these strategies, your food truck business will be well-positioned to grow and scale for long-term success.

Add additional trucks or locations: Adding additional trucks or locations is a great way to scale and grow your food truck business. This can include adding more trucks to your fleet, opening additional locations, or even expanding into brick-and-mortar restaurants. Expanding your reach in this way can help you to reach new customers and tap into new markets.

Leverage social media: Social media can be a powerful tool for scaling and growing your food truck business. Platforms like Facebook, Instagram, and Twitter can help you to connect with customers, promote your business, and build your brand. Use social media to share updates about your business, post pictures of your food, and engage with customers.

Optimize your menu: Optimizing your menu is essential for scaling and growing your food truck business. This includes regularly adding new menu items, experimenting with different recipes, and making changes to your menu based on customer feedback. By optimizing your menu, you can attract new customers, increase sales, and stand out from your competitors.

Develop a customer loyalty program: Developing a customer loyalty program is a great way to scale and grow your food truck business. This includes offering rewards, discounts, or other incentives to customers who frequently visit your food truck. By developing a loyalty program, you can build a loyal customer base and increase repeat business.

Create a mobile app: Creating a mobile app is a great way to scale and grow your food truck business. This can include an ordering app that allows customers to place orders in advance, or a rewards program app that allows customers to earn points and redeem them for discounts or other rewards. By creating a mobile app, you can make it easy for customers to engage with your business and increase sales.

Attend food truck events and festivals: Attending food truck events and festivals is a great way to scale and grow your food truck business. This includes participating in food truck festivals, street fairs, and other events. By attending these events, you can connect with new customers, increase brand awareness, and build your reputation in the food truck industry.

Offer delivery and takeout services: Offering delivery and takeout services is a great way to scale and grow your food truck business. This includes developing partnerships with delivery companies like GrubHub,

DoorDash, and UberEats, or delivering food yourself. By offering delivery and takeout services, you can reach new customers and increase sales.

Build relationships with local suppliers and vendors: Building relationships with local suppliers and vendors is essential for scaling and growing your food truck business. This includes sourcing ingredients from local farms and suppliers, and partnering with vendors who can provide you with the equipment and supplies you need to run your business. By building relationships with local suppliers and vendors, you can lower costs, improve your quality of products, and support local economy.

In conclusion, scaling and growing a food truck business requires a combination of strategy and execution. The strategies listed above are a starting point, but it's important to continuously evaluate and adapt your approach as your business grows and evolves. The key to success is to have a clear vision and plan, to stay adaptable, and to be open to new opportunities and ideas as they arise. By following these steps, you can set your food truck business on the path to long-term growth and success.

Location and Permits: How to find the right location and obtain the necessary permits for your food truck business

Finding the right location and obtaining the necessary permits are crucial steps in starting a successful food truck business. Here are some strategies for finding the right location and obtaining the necessary permits:

Research local laws and regulations: Before setting up your food truck, it's important to research local laws and regulations regarding food truck operations. This includes understanding parking and vending laws, health department regulations, and any other relevant laws in your area.

Identify potential locations: Once you understand the local laws and regulations, you can start identifying potential locations for your food truck. This includes researching areas with high foot traffic, such as downtown areas, parks, and events, as well as areas with less competition from other food trucks and restaurants.

Scout locations in person: Once you've identified potential locations, it's important to scout them in person. This includes visiting the location at different times of day to understand the foot traffic, and evaluating factors such as visibility, accessibility, and safety.

Obtain the necessary permits: Once you've identified the right location for your food truck, it's important to obtain the necessary permits. This includes obtaining a vending permit, a food handling permit, and any other relevant permits required by your local health department or city.

Build relationships with property owners: Building relationships with property owners can help you to secure a location for your food truck. This includes developing relationships with property owners in areas where you would like to operate, and offering to partner with them to promote their business.

Join food truck associations or groups: Joining food truck associations or groups can be a great way to find potential locations and stay up-to-date on regulations. These groups can provide information on local laws, help you connect with other food truck operators, and offer support and resources for running your business.

Get involved in the community: Getting involved in the community can help you to identify potential locations and build relationships with local business owners. This includes participating in community events, supporting local charities, and networking with other businesses.

Keep accurate records: Once you've obtained the necessary permits, it's important to keep accurate records of your permit information, expiration dates, and any other relevant documents. This will help you to stay compliant with local laws and regulations and avoid any potential issues or fines.

Understand parking and vending laws: Parking and vending laws vary from city to city, it's important to understand the laws in your area to avoid any potential issues. This includes understanding the difference between public and private property, and obtaining the necessary permits and licenses to operate on each type of property.

Be aware of health department regulations: Health department regulations are in place to ensure the safety of the food being served. It's important to understand the regulations in your area, including the requirements for food handling and storage, and to maintain a clean and safe food truck.

Be prepared to move locations: As a food truck business owner, you may need to move locations frequently. Be prepared to be flexible and adapt to changes in traffic patterns and local regulations. Having a plan in place for finding new locations and obtaining the necessary permits will help you to quickly adapt to changes.

Consider alternative locations: While traditional locations such as downtown areas and parks may be the most popular, don't overlook alternative locations such as office parks, residential areas, and industrial areas. These locations may have less competition and can be a great way to reach new customers.

In conclusion, finding the right location and obtaining the necessary permits are crucial steps in starting a successful food truck business. Researching local laws and regulations, identifying potential locations, scouting locations in person, obtaining the necessary permits, building relationships with property owners, joining food truck associations or groups, getting involved in the community, keeping accurate records, understanding parking and vending laws, being aware of health department regulations, being prepared to move locations and considering alternative locations are all strategies that can help you to find the right location and obtain the necessary permits for your food truck business. By following these steps, you can set your food truck business on the path to success and navigate the unique challenges of operating a mobile business.

Insurance: How to obtain the necessary insurance to protect your food truck business

Obtaining the necessary insurance to protect your food truck business is a crucial step in starting and running a successful business. Here are some strategies for obtaining the necessary insurance to protect your food truck business:

Understand your risks: Before obtaining insurance, it's important to understand the risks associated with your food truck business. This includes evaluating potential hazards such as food contamination, vehicle accidents, and liability claims.

Research insurance options: Once you've identified the potential risks to your business, research insurance options that can protect you from these risks. This includes researching general liability insurance, commercial auto insurance, workers' compensation insurance, and other relevant policies.

Compare insurance quotes: Compare insurance quotes from multiple providers to ensure you are getting the best coverage at the most competitive price. Be sure to compare policies from different providers, and to evaluate the level of coverage, deductibles and exclusions.

Purchase the appropriate coverage: Once you've compared insurance quotes and identified the best coverage for your business, purchase the appropriate coverage. This includes purchasing general liability insurance to protect your business from liability claims, commercial auto insurance to protect your vehicle, and workers' compensation insurance to protect your employees.

Review and update your insurance coverage: Review and update your insurance coverage on a regular basis. This includes evaluating your coverage needs, re-evaluating your risks, and making any necessary changes to your coverage.

In conclusion, obtaining the necessary insurance to protect your food truck business is a crucial step in starting and running a successful business. Understanding your risks, researching insurance options, comparing insurance quotes, purchasing the appropriate coverage, reviewing and updating your coverage regularly, understanding your policy's limits and exclusions, contacting your insurance agent, understanding the state regulations, considering additional coverage options, and having an emergency plan in place are all strategies that can help you to obtain the necessary insurance to protect your food truck business. By following these steps, you can ensure that your business is protected and that you are prepared for any potential risks or losses.

Understand the difference between policies: Understand the difference between different types of policies. For example, liability insurance covers third-party claims, while a commercial auto policy covers damages to your vehicle. Make sure you have the right type of insurance to protect your business from specific risks.

Keep accurate records: Keep accurate records of your insurance policies, including policy numbers, coverage amounts, and expiration dates. This will help you to stay organized and ensure that your coverage is up-to-date.

Review your coverage annually: Review your coverage annually, and make changes as necessary. This includes re-evaluating your risks, comparing quotes, and adjusting your coverage to meet the changing needs of your business.

Be prepared to demonstrate proof of insurance: Be prepared to demonstrate proof of insurance when requested. This includes carrying proof of insurance with you when operating your food truck and providing proof of insurance to landlords, vendors, and other business partners.

Consider umbrella insurance: Consider umbrella insurance to provide additional liability protection beyond the limits of your standard insurance policies. Umbrella insurance can protect you from large claims and lawsuits.

Understand exclusions and limits: Understand the exclusions and limits of your policies. Some policies may exclude certain types of claims or have limits on the amount of coverage provided. Knowing these exclusions and limits can help you to make informed decisions about your coverage.

Make sure your insurance is up-to-date: Make sure your insurance is up-to-date and that you have adequate coverage. This includes updating your coverage when you make changes to your business, such as adding employees or expanding your operations.

Consider risk management: Consider risk management to help you to identify and mitigate potential risks to your business. This includes developing an emergency plan, implementing safety procedures, and training employees on safe practices.

Be aware of laws and regulations: Be aware of laws and regulations related to insurance for food truck businesses. This includes understanding the insurance requirements in your state and complying with any relevant laws or regulations.

Understand the claims process: Understand the claims process and have the necessary documentation in place in case of an incident or loss. This includes having accurate records of your insurance policies, understanding the steps to file a claim, and being prepared to provide any necessary documentation.

In conclusion, obtaining the necessary insurance to protect your food truck business is an important step in starting and running a successful business. Understanding your risks, researching insurance options, comparing insurance quotes, purchasing the appropriate coverage, reviewing and updating your coverage regularly, understanding your policy's limits and exclusions, contacting your insurance agent, understanding the state regulations, considering additional coverage options, and having an emergency plan in place, understanding the difference between policies, keeping accurate records, reviewing your coverage annually, being prepared to demonstrate proof of insurance, considering umbrella insurance, understanding exclusions and limits, making sure your insurance is up-to-date, considering risk management, being aware of laws and regulations, and understanding the claims process are all strategies that can help you to obtain the necessary insurance to protect your food truck business. By following these steps, you can ensure that your business is protected and that you are prepared for any potential risks or losses.

Social Media and Online Presence: How to use social media and create an online presence to promote your food truck business

Creating a strong social media and online presence is essential for promoting your food truck business and reaching new customers. Here are some strategies for using social media and creating an online presence to promote your food truck business:

Define your target audience: Before creating your social media and online presence, it's important to define your target audience. This includes understanding the demographics, interests, and behavior of your ideal customers, and tailoring your content and messaging to appeal to them.

Establish your brand: Establish your brand by creating a consistent visual identity, tone of voice and messaging across all your social media platforms. This will help you to create a recognizable and memorable brand that customers can easily identify and connect with.

Create a website: Create a website for your food truck business. This will serve as an online hub for your business, where customers can find information about your food truck, menu, location, and more.

Use social media platforms: Use social media platforms such as Facebook, Instagram, Twitter, and TikTok to promote your food truck business. This includes creating engaging content, interacting with customers, and using relevant hashtags to reach new customers.

Use video content: Use video content to promote your food truck business. This includes creating live streams, cooking tutorials, and behind-the-scenes footage to showcase the personality of your business and give customers a glimpse into the daily operations of your food truck.

Use Instagram stories and TikTok: Utilize Instagram stories and TikTok to engage your audience with fun and interactive content. Use polls, Q&A,

and other interactive features to increase engagement and build relationships with your audience.

Create a Google My Business listing: *Create a Google My Business listing for your food truck business. This will help you to appear in local search results and make it easier for customers to find your food truck.*

Use customer reviews: *Use customer reviews to promote your food truck business. This includes encouraging customers to leave reviews on your website, social media platforms, and online directories, and using positive reviews in your marketing materials.*

Use email marketing: *Use email marketing to promote your food truck business. This includes sending newsletters, promotional offers, and updates to customers who have signed up for your email list.*

Use Influencer Marketing: *Utilize influencer marketing by partnering with popular food bloggers, social media personalities and other influencers to promote your food truck business.*

Use Geo-targeting: *Use geo-targeting to reach customers in the specific areas where your food truck operates. This includes using location-based targeting on social media platforms, and focusing on promoting your food truck in the areas where you are located.*

Utilize paid advertising: *Utilize paid advertising on social media platforms and Google Adwords to reach a wider audience and drive more customers to your food truck.*

In conclusion, creating a strong social media and online presence is essential for promoting your food truck business and reaching new customers. Defining your target audience, establishing your brand, creating a website, using social media platforms, using video content, creating a Google My Business listing, using customer reviews, using email marketing, using influencer marketing, using geo-targeting, and utilizing paid advertising are all strategies that can help you to use social media and create an online presence to promote your food truck business. By following these steps, you can reach a wider audience and build relationships with customers, helping to drive more business to your food truck.

Monitor and analyze your social media metrics: Monitor and analyze your social media metrics to understand the performance of your social media campaigns and to identify opportunities for improvement. This includes monitoring engagement, reach, and click-through rates, as well as tracking your website traffic and conversion rates.

Optimize your website for SEO: Optimize your website for SEO to improve your visibility in search engine results and to increase your website traffic. This includes using relevant keywords, creating high-quality content, and building backlinks to your website.

Use social media for customer service: Use social media as a customer service platform to respond to customer inquiries and to address any customer complaints or concerns. This can help to improve customer satisfaction and to build trust with your audience.

Use social media for market research: Use social media for market research to understand your customers and to identify new opportunities for your business. This includes tracking trends, monitoring customer sentiment, and analyzing competitor activity.

Use social media to build relationships: Use social media to build relationships with your customers by engaging with them and by providing valuable content. This can help to build loyalty and to turn customers into brand advocates.

Use social media to create events: Use social media to create events and to promote them. This includes creating virtual events, such as cooking classes or live Q&A sessions, and promoting them through social media platforms.

Use social media to offer promotions and discounts: Use social media to offer promotions and discounts to attract customers to your food truck. This can include offering a discount on your menu items, hosting a contest, or giving away free items.

Use social media to share customer testimonials: Use social media to share customer testimonials to build trust and credibility with your audience. This includes sharing positive reviews and feedback from customers on your social media platforms.

In conclusion, creating a strong social media and online presence is essential for promoting your food truck business and reaching new customers. By monitoring and analyzing your social media metrics, optimizing your website for SEO, using social media for customer service, using social media for market research, building relationships, creating events, offering promotions and discounts, and sharing customer testimonials, you can use social media and create an online presence to promote your food truck business. By following these strategies, you can increase visibility, engagement, and drive more customers to your food truck, ultimately leading to more success for your business.

Customer Service: How to provide excellent customer service to attract and retain customers

Providing excellent customer service is essential for attracting and retaining customers in any business, and food truck businesses are no exception. Here are some strategies for providing excellent customer service to attract and retain customers in your food truck business:

Train your staff: Train your staff on the importance of customer service and how to provide it. This includes training them on how to handle customer complaints, how to provide a positive customer experience, and how to build relationships with customers.

Create a customer-focused culture: Create a customer-focused culture within your food truck business. This includes making customer service a priority, encouraging customer feedback, and recognizing and rewarding employees for excellent customer service.

Be responsive and accessible: Be responsive and accessible to your customers. This includes answering customer inquiries in a timely manner, providing accurate and helpful information, and being available to assist customers when they need it.

Listen and empathize: Listen and empathize with your customers. This includes understanding their needs and concerns, and showing that you care about their experience.

Be flexible and adaptable: Be flexible and adaptable to your customers' needs. This includes offering customized menu items, accommodating up orders, and going out of your way to accommodate special requests.

Use customer feedback to improve: Use customer feedback to improve your customer service. This includes soliciting feedback from customers, analyzing feedback data, and taking action to address any issues or concerns that customers have.

Create a loyalty program: Create a loyalty program to reward customers for their repeat business. This can include offering discounts, special promotions, or other incentives to customers who visit your food truck frequently.

Follow up with customers: Follow up with customers after their visit to your food truck. This can include sending a survey, an email or a message on social media, to understand their experience and see if there's anything you can improve.

Use social media to engage with customers: Use social media to engage with customers and to provide excellent customer service. This includes responding to customer inquiries and comments, addressing customer complaints, and providing helpful information and resources.

Create a sense of community: Create a sense of community around your food truck by hosting events, creating a customer appreciation day, or participating in local community events.

Keep your promises: Keep your promises to customers by following through on any commitments you make to them. This includes honoring any guarantees, discounts or specials you offer, and delivering on any promises you make.

Be honest and transparent: Be honest and transparent with your customers. This includes being upfront about any delays or issues that may arise, and providing accurate

and honest information about your menu, ingredients, and pricing.

Use technology to enhance customer service: Use technology to enhance customer service. This can include implementing an online ordering system, using a mobile app to track orders, or using a customer relationship management (CRM) system to keep track of customer interactions and preferences.

Personalize the customer experience: Personalize the customer experience by remembering customer's names, preferences, and order history. This can help to build a relationship with your customers and make them feel valued.

Provide exceptional service during peak hours: Provide exceptional service during peak hours. This can include having extra staff on hand, providing expedited service, and ensuring that you have enough inventory to meet demand.

Make it easy for customers to reach out: Make it easy for customers to reach out to you with questions, comments, or concerns. This includes providing clear contact information, responding promptly to customer inquiries, and making it easy for customers to leave feedback.

Continuously improve: Continuously improve your customer service by evaluating your processes, seeking feedback, and making changes as needed. This includes regularly training your staff, updating your procedures, and incorporating new technologies to enhance the customer experience.

In conclusion, providing excellent customer service is essential for attracting and retaining customers in your food truck business. By training your staff, creating a customer-focused culture, being responsive and accessible, listening and empathizing with customers, being flexible and adaptable, using customer feedback to improve, creating a loyalty program, following up with customers, engaging with customers on social media, creating a sense of community, keeping promises, being honest and transparent, using technology to enhance customer service, personalizing the customer experience, providing exceptional service during peak hours, and continuously improving your customer service, you can ensure that your customers have a positive experience and are more likely to return to your food truck. By following these strategies, you can increase customer satisfaction, build relationships, and ultimately drive more business to your food truck.

Menu and Food Cost: How to develop a profitable menu and manage food cost

Developing a profitable menu and managing food cost is critical for the success of any food truck business. Here are some strategies for developing a profitable menu and managing food cost:

Understand your target market: Understand your target market and create a menu that appeals to them. This includes researching what types of food and flavors are popular in your area, and tailoring your menu to meet the needs and preferences of your customers.

Create a balance of items: Create a balance of items on your menu by including a variety of options, such as appetizers, entrees, sides, and desserts. This will help to appeal to a broader range of customers and increase the chances of them finding something they like.

Keep it simple: Keep your menu simple by offering a limited number of items. This will make it easier for you to manage your inventory, reduce food waste, and increase efficiency in the kitchen.

Use seasonal ingredients: Use seasonal ingredients to create a menu that changes with the seasons. This can help to reduce food cost and increase the appeal of your menu by offering fresh and unique options.

Use cost-effective ingredients: Use cost-effective ingredients to help manage food cost. This includes using ingredients that are in season, sourcing ingredients from local suppliers, and using bulk-purchasing to reduce the cost of ingredients.

Test your menu items: Test your menu items before adding them to the menu. This includes conducting customer taste tests, and gathering feedback to determine which items are popular and which are not.

Plan your menu around your food cost: Plan your menu around your food cost by determining the cost of each menu item, and pricing them accordingly. This includes analyzing the cost of ingredients, labor, and overhead, and using this information to determine the optimal price for each menu item.

Track your food cost: Track your food cost by keeping accurate records of your inventory and sales. This includes monitoring your food cost percentage, and taking steps to reduce it when it's too high.

Use technology to manage food cost: Use technology to manage food cost. This includes using software to track inventory, sales, and food cost, and using tools such as recipe costing software to calculate the cost of each menu item.

Monitor your competition: Monitor your competition to understand their menu offerings, pricing and promotions. This will allow you to adjust your menu and pricing accordingly to stay competitive in the market.

Consider portion control: Consider portion control to help manage food cost. This includes determining the appropriate portion size for each menu item, and training your staff to serve the correct portions.

Be mindful of food waste: Be mindful of food waste by implementing a food waste reduction program. This includes monitoring food waste, identifying areas where waste can be reduced, and taking steps to reduce waste in the kitchen.

Continuously evaluate and adjust your menu: Continuously evaluate and adjust your menu based on customer feedback, sales data, and food cost data. This includes regularly removing low-performing items, and introducing new items to keep your menu fresh and appealing.

In conclusion, developing a profitable menu and managing food cost is critical for the success of any food truck business. By understanding your target market, creating a balance of items, keeping it simple, using seasonal ingredients, using cost-effective ingredients, testing your menu items, planning your menu around your food cost, tracking your food cost, using technology to manage food cost, monitoring your competition, considering portion control, being mindful of food waste, and continuously evaluating and adjusting your menu, you can help to ensure that your menu is profitable and that you are effectively managing your food cost. Additionally, it is important to regularly review your menu items and pricing, and make adjustments as needed. This can include removing items that are not selling well, introducing new items, and adjusting prices to better reflect the cost of ingredients and labor.

Another important aspect to consider is your food cost percentage, which is the percentage of the selling price that goes towards the cost of food. A common industry standard is to aim for a food cost percentage of around 28-35%. By monitoring and controlling your food cost percentage, you can ensure that you are making a profit on your menu items and that your food truck business is sustainable in the long run.

It's also important to consider the cost of labor, which includes the cost of your staff, when developing your menu. Be mindful of how much time it takes to prepare each menu item, and how many staff members are needed to prepare it. This will help you to price your menu items appropriately, so that you can cover your labor costs and still make a profit.

Finally, menu engineering is an important aspect of menu development. This includes analyzing sales data, customer feedback, and menu popularity, to understand which menu items are driving profit and which are not. By understanding which menu items are your most profitable, you can focus on promoting these items and make adjustments to non-performing items to improve sales and profitability.

In conclusion, developing a profitable menu and managing food cost is an ongoing process that requires regular review, analysis, and adjustments. By understanding your target market, creating a balance of items, keeping it simple, using seasonal ingredients, using cost-effective ingredients, testing your menu items, planning your menu around your food cost, tracking your food cost, using technology to manage food cost, monitoring your competition, considering portion control, being mindful of food waste, continuously evaluating and adjusting your menu, and using menu engineering, you can create a profitable menu and effectively manage food cost for your food truck business.

Food Truck Design and Branding: How to design and brand your food truck to stand out in the market

Designing and branding your food truck is an essential aspect of standing out in the market and attracting customers. Here are some strategies for designing and branding your food truck to make it stand out in the market:

Develop a unique concept and brand: Develop a unique concept and brand for your food truck. This includes determining your target market, identifying your unique selling proposition, and creating a brand that reflects the values and personality of your food truck.

Design the exterior of your food truck: Design the exterior of your food truck to make it visually appealing and memorable. This includes using colors, graphics, and branding elements that reflect your concept and brand, and that are easy to read and recognize from a distance.

Design the interior of your food truck: Design the interior of your food truck to create a comfortable and inviting space for customers. This includes using colors, lighting, and decor that reflects your concept and brand, and that makes it easy for customers to navigate and order food.

Use technology to enhance the customer experience: Use technology to enhance the customer experience, such as digital menu boards, QR codes, and mobile ordering. This can help to streamline the ordering process, reduce wait times, and provide a more engaging and interactive experience for customers.

Create a mobile website: Create a mobile website for your food truck that includes information about your menu, location, and hours of operation. This can help to make it easy for customers to find and order from your food truck.

Use social media to promote your food truck: Use social media to promote your food truck, including creating a profile for your food truck on popular social media platforms, and regularly posting updates, pictures, and promotions to attract customers.

Create a distinct logo and tagline: Create a distinct logo and tagline for your food truck that reflects your concept and brand, and that is easy to recognize and remember. This can help to make your food truck more memorable and increase brand awareness.

Utilize packaging and uniforms: Utilize packaging and uniforms to create a consistent and professional image for your food truck. This includes using packaging and uniforms that reflect your concept and brand, and that make it easy for customers to identify and remember your food truck.

Create a loyalty program: Create a loyalty program to reward customers for their repeat business. This can include offering discounts, special promotions, or other incentives to customers who visit your food truck frequently.

Participate in food truck events and festivals: Participate in food truck events and festivals to increase visibility and attract new customers. This includes promoting your food truck at events, offering special menu items, and providing a fun and engaging experience for customers.

Build a community around your food truck: Build a community around your food truck by hosting events, creating a customer appreciation day, or participating in local community events. This can help to create a sense of loyalty and encourage customers to return to your food truck.

Use Vehicle Wraps or decals: Use vehicle wraps or decals to make your food truck more eye-catching and memorable. This can help to increase brand awareness and make it easy for customers to find and remember your food truck.

In conclusion, designing and branding your food truck is an essential aspect of standing out in the market and attracting customers. By developing a unique concept and brand, designing the exterior and interior of your food truck, using technology to enhance the customer experience, creating a mobile website, using social media to promote your food truck, creating a distinct logo and tagline, utilizing packaging and uniforms, creating a loyalty program, participating in food truck events and festivals, building a community

around your food truck, and using vehicle wraps or decals, you can make your food truck more visually appealing, memorable, and professional. Additionally, it is important to maintain consistency in your branding and design across all platforms, including your food truck, website, social media, packaging, and uniforms. This will help to create a strong and recognizable brand that customers can easily associate with your food truck.

Another important aspect to consider is the functionality of your food truck design. This includes creating a user-friendly layout, making sure that the kitchen and service areas are efficient, and that the food truck is easy to clean and maintain. By designing a functional and efficient food truck, you can improve the customer experience, increase efficiency in the kitchen, and reduce operational costs.

It's also important to consider the mobility and ease of use when designing your food truck. This includes making sure that the food truck is easy to maneuver, park, and set up. By designing a mobile and easy-to-use food truck, you can improve the flexibility of your business and increase your ability to reach customers in different locations.

Finally, it's important to keep in mind the regulations and rules of your local area when designing your food truck. This includes making sure that your food truck meets the necessary health and safety requirements, as well as any regulations related to parking and operation. By following the regulations, you can avoid any legal issues and ensure that your food truck is compliant.

In conclusion, designing and branding your food truck is an essential aspect of standing out in the market and attracting customers. By developing a unique concept and brand, designing the exterior and interior of your food truck, using technology to enhance the customer experience, creating a mobile website, using social media to promote your food truck, creating a distinct logo and tagline, utilizing packaging and uniforms, creating a loyalty program, participating in food truck events and festivals, building a community around your food truck, and using vehicle wraps or decals, and keeping in mind the regulations and rules of your local area, you can make your food truck more visually appealing, memorable, professional, functional, mobile, and compliant to the regulations. By following these strategies, you can increase visibility and attract more customers to your food truck business.

Another important aspect to consider is the use of lighting in your food truck design. Proper lighting can enhance the ambiance and atmosphere of your food truck, making it more inviting and appealing to customers. This can include using exterior lighting to make your food truck more visible at night, and interior lighting to create a warm and inviting atmosphere. Additionally, you can also use lighting to highlight certain areas of your food truck, such as menu boards or branding elements.

Another way to stand out in the market is to offer unique and specialty items on your menu. This can include offering unique flavor combinations, using locally sourced ingredients, or creating signature dishes that are only available at your food truck. Offering unique and specialty items can help to differentiate your food truck from others and attract customers who are looking for something different.

Customer service is also crucial to the success of a food truck business. Providing excellent customer service can help to create a positive reputation and attract repeat customers. This can include providing friendly and efficient service, accommodating up the food quickly, resolving customer complaints, and going above and beyond to make sure that customers are satisfied.

Finally, it's important to continuously evaluate and improve your food truck design and branding. This can include gathering customer feedback, analyzing sales data, and staying up to date with current trends in the food truck industry. By continuously evaluating and improving your food truck design and branding, you can ensure that your food truck stays relevant and attractive to customers.

In conclusion, designing and branding your food truck is an ongoing process that requires regular review, analysis, and adjustments. By developing a unique concept and brand, designing the exterior and interior of your food truck, using technology to enhance the customer experience, creating a mobile website, using social media to promote your food truck, creating a distinct logo and tagline, utilizing packaging and uniforms, creating a loyalty program, participating in food truck events and festivals, building a community around your food truck, using vehicle wraps or decals, keeping in mind the regulations and rules of your local area, using lighting to enhance the ambiance, offering unique and specialty items on your menu, providing excellent customer service, and continuously evaluating and improving your food truck design and branding, you can make your food truck more visually appealing, memorable, professional, functional, mobile, and compliant to the regulations. These strategies can help you to increase visibility, attract more customers, and stand out in the market.

Food Truck Festivals and Events: How to participate in food truck festivals and events to increase visibility and generate revenue

Participating in food truck festivals and events can be a great way to increase visibility and generate revenue for your food truck business. Here are some strategies for participating in food truck festivals and events:

Research and select the right events: Research and select food truck festivals and events that align with your target market and that are likely to attract a high number of attendees. Consider the location, demographics, and reputation of the event before committing to participate.

Plan ahead and prepare: Plan ahead and prepare for the event by creating a detailed schedule, ordering necessary supplies, and preparing your staff. Make sure that you have all necessary permits, licenses, and insurance in place, and that your food truck is in good working condition.

Optimize your menu: Optimize your menu for the event by offering a mix of popular items, as well as new and unique items that you can promote. Keep in mind the event theme, the audience and the weather.

Promote your participation: Promote your participation in the event on social media, your website, and other marketing channels. Use the event's hashtags and create a buzz around your participation.

Create a visually appealing setup: Create a visually appealing setup at the event by using banners, flags, and other branding elements that reflect your concept and brand. Use lighting and decor to create a warm and inviting atmosphere.

Provide excellent customer service: Provide excellent customer service at the event by being friendly, efficient, and accommodating up the food quickly. Be prepared to handle any customer complaints or concerns.

Collect customer information: Collect customer information at the event, such as contact information and feedback, to use for future marketing and promotions.

Take advantage of the event's marketing: Take advantage of the event's marketing efforts by participating in the event's social media campaigns, contests and giveaways.

Network with other food truck businesses: Network with other food truck businesses at the event to share ideas and best practices, and to make connections for future events.

Use the event as an opportunity to test new menu items and concepts: Use the event as an opportunity to test new menu items and concepts, and gather feedback from customers.

Follow up with customers after the event: Follow up with customers after the event by sending thank you emails, surveys, and special offers to encourage repeat business.

Participate in multiple events: Participate in multiple events throughout the year to increase visibility and revenue.

Participating in food truck festivals and events can be a great way to increase visibility and generate revenue for your food truck business. By researching and selecting the right events, planning ahead and preparing, optimizing your menu, promoting your participation, creating a visually appealing setup, providing excellent customer service, collecting customer information, taking advantage of the event's marketing, networking with other food truck businesses, using the event as an opportunity to test new menu items and concepts, following up with customers after the event, and participating in multiple events throughout the year, you can increase visibility, generate revenue, and build a loyal customer base for your food truck business.

It's also important to keep in mind the costs associated with participating in food truck festivals and events. This includes the cost of the event fee, the cost of supplies, and the cost of labor. Be sure to factor these costs into your budget and ensure that you have enough funds to cover them.

Additionally, you may also want to consider offering special deals or promotions to attract customers and generate more revenue.

Another important aspect to consider is the competition at the event. It's important to research the other food truck businesses that will be participating and to consider how you can stand out and attract customers. This can include offering unique menu items, providing exceptional customer service, or having a visually appealing setup.

It's also important to have a solid plan for the event, such as having a designated person in charge, having a schedule of when staff should arrive and depart, and having a plan for dealing with any unexpected issues that may arise.

Finally, it's important to have a plan for after the event. This includes following up with customers, analyzing sales data, and evaluating the event's success. This can help you to make adjustments for future events and to improve your overall performance.

In conclusion, participating in food truck festivals and events can be a great way to increase visibility and generate revenue for your food truck business. By researching and selecting the right events, planning ahead and preparing, optimizing your menu, promoting your participation, creating a visually appealing setup, providing excellent customer service, collecting customer information, taking advantage of the event's marketing, networking with other food truck businesses, using the event as an opportunity to test new menu items and concepts, following up with customers after the event, and participating in multiple events throughout the year, it's important to also consider the costs, the competition, and the plan before, during and after the event, and have a plan for dealing with any unexpected issues that may arise. These strategies can help you to increase visibility, generate revenue, and build a loyal customer base for your food truck business.

Another important aspect to consider when participating in food truck festivals and events is to make sure you have an efficient and organized process for taking orders and payments. This can include using a mobile POS system, having a clear menu board, and having a system for handling cash and credit card transactions. By having an efficient and organized process, you can improve the customer experience and reduce wait times.

Another way to increase visibility and generate revenue at food truck festivals and events is to offer catering services. This can include offering catering for private events, parties, and corporate events. By offering catering services, you can expand your customer base and generate additional revenue streams.

It's also important to be prepared for different weather conditions when participating in food truck festivals and events. This can include having a plan for dealing with rain, extreme heat or cold, and other weather-related issues. This can include having tarps or canopies to protect your food truck, having fans or heaters to keep customers comfortable, and having a plan for dealing with power outages.

Finally, it's important to have a plan for dealing with any unexpected issues that may arise when participating in food truck festivals and events. This can include having a designated person in charge, having a plan for dealing with unexpected repairs or maintenance, and having a contingency plan for dealing with unexpected weather conditions.

In conclusion, participating in food truck festivals and events can be a great way to increase visibility and generate revenue for your food truck business. By researching and selecting the right events, planning ahead and preparing, optimizing your menu, promoting your participation, creating a visually appealing setup, providing excellent customer service, collecting customer information, taking advantage of the event's marketing, networking with other food truck businesses, using the event as an opportunity to test new menu items and concepts, following up with customers after the event, and participating in multiple events throughout the year, it's important to also consider having an efficient and organized process for taking orders and payments, offering catering services, being prepared for different weather conditions and having a plan for dealing with any unexpected issues that may arise. By following these strategies, you can increase visibility, generate revenue, and build a loyal customer base for your food truck business.

Another strategy for increasing visibility and generating revenue at food truck festivals and events is to partner with local businesses. This can include partnering with breweries, wineries, or other local food vendors to create unique and exclusive offerings for customers. By partnering with local businesses, you can tap into their customer base and generate additional revenue streams.

It's also important to consider the impact of your food truck on the environment when participating in food truck festivals and events. This can include using eco-friendly packaging, recycling or composting food waste, and using energy-efficient equipment. By being environmentally conscious, you can appeal to customers who are looking for sustainable and green options, and also contribute to the community and the environment.

It's also important to stay up-to-date with the regulations and laws regarding food trucks in your area. This can include obtaining the necessary permits and licenses, adhering to food safety regulations, and being aware of any parking or zoning restrictions. By staying compliant with regulations and laws, you can avoid fines and penalties, and avoid any legal troubles that can affect the success of your food truck business.

Finally, to increase visibility and generate revenue, it's important to stay active and engaged with your customers. This can include regularly updating your social media accounts, responding to customer feedback, and offering loyalty programs or rewards to customers. By staying active and engaged with your customers, you can create a positive reputation, attract repeat customers, and generate additional revenue streams.

In conclusion, participating in food truck festivals and events can be a great way to increase visibility and generate revenue for your food truck business. By researching and selecting the right events, planning ahead and preparing, optimizing your menu, promoting your participation, creating a visually appealing setup, providing excellent customer service, collecting customer information, taking advantage of the event's marketing, networking with other food truck businesses, using the event as an opportunity to test new menu items and concepts, following up with customers after the event, and participating in multiple events throughout the year, it's important to also consider partnering with local businesses, being environmentally conscious, staying up-to-date with regulations and laws, and staying active and engaged with your customers. By following these strategies, you can increase visibility, generate revenue, and build a loyal customer base for your food truck business.

Food Truck Associations and Networks: How to join food truck associations and networks to connect with other food truck business owners

Joining food truck associations and networks can be a valuable way for food truck business owners to connect with other food truck business owners, gain access to resources and support, and stay informed about industry trends and regulations. Here are some strategies for joining food truck associations and networks:

Research and select the right associations and networks: Research and select food truck associations and networks that align with your goals and that offer the resources and support that you need. Consider the location, focus, and reputation of the association or network before committing to join.

Understand the benefits and costs: Understand the benefits and costs of joining a food truck association or network. Benefits can include access to resources, support, networking opportunities, and discounts on products and services. Costs can include membership fees and dues.

Attend events and networking opportunities: Attend events and networking opportunities offered by the association or network to connect with other food truck business owners and gain valuable insights and advice.

Get involved and volunteer: Get involved and volunteer with the association or network to gain leadership experience and to make valuable connections within the food truck industry.

Stay informed about industry trends and regulations: Stay informed about industry trends and regulations by reading the association or network's publications, newsletters and attending their seminars.

Leverage the association or network's reputation: Leverage the reputation of the association or network to build credibility and attract customers.

Take advantage of the association or network's marketing efforts: Take advantage of the association or network's marketing efforts by participating in their social media campaigns, contests and giveaways.

Collaborate with other food truck businesses: Collaborate with other food truck businesses in the association or network to share ideas, best practices, and to create new opportunities for growth and expansion.

Be an active member: Be an active member of the association or network by participating in events, attending meetings, and contributing to discussions and decision-making processes.

Use the association or network's resources: Use the association or network's resources, such as legal and financial advice, to help your food truck business thrive.

Be a mentor: Be a mentor for new members and share your knowledge and experience to help them succeed.

Take advantage of the association or network's advocacy efforts: Take advantage of the association or network's advocacy efforts by participating in lobbying and grassroots campaigns to improve the food truck industry.

Joining food truck associations and networks can be a valuable way for food truck business owners to connect with other food truck business owners, gain access to resources and support, and stay informed about industry trends and regulations. By researching and selecting the right associations and networks, understanding the benefits and costs, attending events and networking opportunities, getting involved and volunteering, staying informed about industry trends and regulations, leveraging the association or network's reputation, taking advantage of the association or network's marketing efforts, collaborating with other food truck businesses, being an active member, using the association or network's resources, being a mentor, and taking advantage of the association or network's advocacy efforts, food truck business owners can connect with other food truck business owners, gain access to resources and support, and stay informed about industry trends and regulations to grow and expand their food truck business.

Another important aspect of joining food truck associations and networks is the ability to access networking and partnership opportunities. By connecting with other food truck business owners, you can collaborate on promotions, events, and menu offerings. This can help to increase visibility and generate revenue for your food truck business.

Another benefit of joining food truck associations and networks is the ability to access resources and support. This can include access to legal and financial advice, training and education, and access to industry-specific products and services. This can help to improve the efficiency and effectiveness of your food truck business, and can also help to reduce costs.

Another benefit of joining food truck associations and networks is the ability to stay informed about industry trends and regulations. This can include staying informed about new laws and regulations, industry trends, and best practices. By staying informed, you can make informed decisions and adjust your business strategies accordingly.

Finally, by joining food truck associations and networks, you can contribute to the advocacy and development of the food truck industry. By participating in lobbying and grassroots campaigns, you can help to improve the food truck industry and create a more favorable environment for food truck businesses to thrive.

In conclusion, joining food truck associations and networks can be a valuable way for food truck business owners to connect with other food truck business owners, gain access to resources and support, stay informed about industry trends and regulations, and contribute to the advocacy and development of the food truck industry. By researching and selecting the right associations and networks, understanding the benefits and costs, attending events and networking opportunities, getting involved and volunteering, staying informed about industry trends and regulations, leveraging the association or network's reputation, taking advantage of the association or network's marketing efforts, collaborating with other food truck businesses, being an active member, using the association or network's resources, being a mentor, and taking advantage of the association or network's advocacy efforts, food truck business owners can access networking and partnership opportunities, access resources and support, stay informed about industry trends and regulations, and contribute to the advocacy and development of the food truck industry to grow and expand their food truck business.

Another key benefit of joining food truck associations and networks is the ability to access industry-specific training and education. These can include workshops, webinars, seminars, and other educational opportunities that can help food truck business owners to improve their knowledge and skills in areas such as food safety, business management, marketing, and customer service. This can help to improve the overall quality of your food truck business and enable you to offer a better customer experience.

Additionally, by joining food truck associations and networks, you can gain access to industry-specific products and services at discounted prices. This can include things like equipment, supplies, and insurance. This can help to reduce costs and improve the efficiency of your food truck business.

Another benefit of joining food truck associations and networks is the ability to access mentorship and guidance from more experienced food truck business owners. These individuals can provide valuable insights and advice on how to navigate the food truck industry, and can also offer support and guidance on specific business challenges.

Finally, by joining food truck associations and networks, you can contribute to the development and growth of the food truck industry as a whole. This can include participating in initiatives and programs that help to promote and support the food truck industry, such as industry events, food truck festivals, and lobbying efforts.

In conclusion, joining food truck associations and networks can be a valuable way for food truck business owners to connect with other food truck business owners, gain access to resources and support, stay informed about industry trends and regulations, and contribute to the advocacy and development of the food truck industry. By researching and selecting the right associations and networks, understanding the benefits and costs, attending events and networking opportunities, getting involved and volunteering, staying informed about industry trends and regulations, leveraging the association or network's reputation, taking advantage of the association or network's marketing efforts, collaborating with other food truck businesses, being an active member, using the association or network's resources, being a mentor, accessing industry-specific training and education, gaining access to discounted industry-specific products and services, having mentorship and guidance from more experienced business owners and contributing to the development and growth of the food truck industry as a whole, food truck business owners can improve the overall quality and efficiency of their business, and help to promote and support the growth of the food truck industry.

Food Truck Safety and Maintenance: How to maintain your vehicle and equipment to ensure safety and longevity

Maintaining your food truck's vehicle and equipment is crucial to ensuring safety and longevity. Here are some strategies for food truck safety and maintenance:

Regularly Inspect and Service Your Vehicle: Regularly inspect and service your vehicle to ensure that it is in good working condition. This can include regular oil changes, tire rotations, and brake inspections. It's also important to have your vehicle serviced by a qualified mechanic who is familiar with food trucks and their specific needs.

Keep Your Food Truck Clean: Keep your food truck clean by regularly washing the exterior, interior, and equipment. This can help to prevent the buildup of dirt and grime, which can lead to equipment failure and safety hazards.

Regularly Inspect and Service Your Equipment: Regularly inspect and service your equipment to ensure that it is in good working condition. This can include regular cleaning, oiling, and lubrication of equipment. It's also important to have your equipment serviced by a qualified technician who is familiar with food truck equipment and their specific needs.

Follow Food Safety Guidelines: Follow food safety guidelines to prevent foodborne illness. This can include keeping hot foods hot and cold foods cold, properly storing and handling food, and regularly cleaning and sanitizing equipment.

Regularly Check and Maintain Your Plumbing and Electrical Systems: Regularly check and maintain your plumbing and electrical systems to ensure that they are in good working condition. This can include checking for leaks, testing electrical connections, and ensuring that all systems are up to code.

Keep Your Food Truck in Compliance with Regulations: Keep your food truck in compliance with regulations by obtaining the necessary permits and licenses, and adhering to food safety regulations. By staying compliant with regulations, you can avoid fines and penalties, and avoid any legal troubles that can affect the success of your food truck business.

Have an emergency plan: Have an emergency plan in case of breakdowns or other emergencies. This can include having a backup generator, a list of emergency contact numbers, and a plan of action in case of equipment failure or other emergencies.

Have a Preventative Maintenance Schedule: Have a preventative maintenance schedule in place to ensure that your vehicle and equipment are regularly inspected and serviced. This can help to prevent breakdowns and equipment failure, and can also help to prolong the life of your vehicle and equipment.

Keep Records of Maintenance and Repairs: Keep records of maintenance and repairs to your vehicle and equipment. This can help to identify patterns of wear and tear, and can also help to identify potential issues before they become major problems.

Invest in High-Quality Equipment: Invest in high-quality equipment to ensure that your food truck is safe and reliable. High-quality equipment can be more expensive initially, but it can also last longer, require less maintenance, and reduce the risk of equipment failure.

In conclusion, maintaining your food truck's vehicle and equipment is crucial to ensuring safety and longevity. By regularly inspecting and servicing your vehicle, keeping your food truck clean, regularly inspecting and servicing your equipment, following food safety guidelines, regularly checking and maintaining your plumbing and electrical systems, keeping your food truck in compliance with regulations, having an emergency plan, having a preventative maintenance schedule, keeping records of maintenance and repairs and investing in high-quality equipment, food truck business owners can ensure that their vehicle and equipment are in good working condition, prevent breakdowns and equipment failure, and prolong the life of their vehicle and equipment to ensure safety and longevity of their business.

Another important aspect of food truck safety and maintenance is training for staff. This can include training on proper food handling, sanitation and safety protocols, as well as training on how to properly operate and maintain equipment. This can help to ensure that staff are aware of potential hazards and know how to prevent and respond to incidents.

Another important consideration is having a regular schedule for deep cleaning and sanitizing the food truck. This can include cleaning and sanitizing surfaces, equipment, and storage areas to prevent the spread of bacteria and other contaminants.

Another important aspect is the regular check-up of the vehicle's tires, brakes, and fluid levels. This can help to ensure that the vehicle is roadworthy and can safely transport food and equipment.

In addition to regular maintenance, it's important to have a plan in place for unexpected repairs and maintenance needs. This can include having a list of trusted mechanics and repair shops, as well as a budget set aside for unexpected repairs.

Finally, it's important to have an emergency plan in case of accidents or incidents. This can include having emergency contact numbers readily available, having first aid kits on hand, and having an evacuation plan in case of an emergency.

In conclusion, maintaining your food truck's vehicle and equipment is crucial to ensuring safety and longevity. By regularly inspecting and servicing your vehicle, keeping your food truck clean, regularly inspecting and servicing your equipment, following food safety guidelines, regularly checking and maintaining your plumbing and electrical systems, keeping your food truck in compliance with regulations, having an emergency plan, having a preventative maintenance schedule, keeping records of maintenance and repairs, investing in high-quality equipment, training staff on proper food handling, sanitation and safety protocols, having a regular schedule for deep cleaning and sanitizing the food truck, checking the vehicle's tires, brakes, and fluid levels, having a plan in place for unexpected repairs and maintenance needs and having an emergency plan in case of accidents or incidents, food truck business owners can ensure that their vehicle and equipment are in good working condition, prevent breakdowns and equipment failure, and prolong the life of their vehicle and equipment to ensure safety and longevity of their business.

Mobile Payment and Point of Sale Systems: How to choose and implement mobile payment and point of sale systems for your food truck business

Mobile payment and point of sale (POS) systems are an important aspect of running a food truck business. These systems allow customers to make payments quickly and easily, and can also provide valuable data and insights into sales and customer behavior. Here are some strategies for choosing and implementing mobile payment and POS systems for your food truck business:

Research different systems: Research different mobile payment and POS systems to find the one that best fits your business needs. Look for systems that are user-friendly, easy to set up and use, and have a wide range of features and integrations.

Consider compatibility: Consider compatibility when choosing a mobile payment and POS system. Make sure that the system is compatible with your existing equipment and software, such as your accounting software, inventory management system, and customer management system.

Look for scalability: Look for a mobile payment and POS system that is scalable. As your business grows, you'll want a system that can grow with you and handle an increasing number of transactions and customers.

Evaluate the cost: Evaluate the cost of different mobile payment and POS systems. Compare the cost of the system, as well as any additional costs such as transaction fees or monthly fees.

Check for security features: Check for security features when choosing a mobile payment and POS system. Look for systems that have built-in security features such as encryption, fraud detection, and data backup.

Test the system before implementing: Test the system before implementing it in your food truck business. This will give you an opportunity to familiarize yourself with the system and ensure that it is functioning properly.

Provide training for staff: Provide training for staff on how to use the new system. This will ensure that they are able to assist customers with payments and troubleshoot any issues that may arise.

Integrate with marketing and customer relationship management tools: Integrate your mobile payment and POS system with marketing and customer relationship management tools. This will allow you to track customer behavior, create targeted marketing campaigns, and improve customer loyalty.

Consider mobile payments: Consider offering mobile payments such as Apple Pay or Google Wallet. This can help to attract customers who prefer to pay with their mobile devices.

Monitor and analyze data: Monitor and analyze data from your mobile payment and POS system to gain insights into sales and customer behavior. This data can help you make informed decisions about your food truck business, such as adjusting menu prices or promoting certain menu items.

In conclusion, choosing and implementing mobile payment and POS systems for your food truck business is an important aspect of running a food truck business. By researching different systems, considering compatibility, looking for scalability, evaluating the cost, checking for security features, testing the system before implementing, providing training for staff, integrating with marketing and customer relationship management tools, offering mobile payments, and monitoring and analyzing data, food truck business owners can find the best system for their business, ensure that the system is functional and secure, and gain valuable insights into sales and customer behavior to improve their business.

Mobile Payment and Point of Sale Systems: How to choose and implement mobile payment and point of sale systems for your food truck business

Mobile payment and point of sale (POS) systems are becoming increasingly important for food truck businesses as they provide convenience and efficiency for customers and business owners alike. Here are some additional strategies for choosing and implementing mobile payment and POS systems for your food truck business:

Choose a system that is cloud-based: Cloud-based systems offer the ability to access your data and manage your business from anywhere, allowing for more flexibility and ease of use.

Look for a system that offers inventory management: An inventory management feature allows you to track the stock of your ingredients, which is important for forecasting and maintaining a consistent menu.

Check for integrations with accounting software: Integrations with accounting software such as QuickBooks or Xero can help to streamline your financial management and save time on bookkeeping.

Consider a system that has a built-in customer database: A customer database feature allows you to store customer information and purchase history, which can be used to create targeted marketing campaigns and improve customer loyalty.

Look for a system that offers real-time reporting and analytics: Real-time reporting and analytics can provide valuable insights into sales trends, customer behavior, and inventory management, allowing you to make data-driven decisions for your business.

Choose a system that offers a mobile app: A mobile app allows customers to place orders and make payments directly from their mobile devices, which can speed up the ordering process and improve customer convenience.

Consider a system that offers multiple payment options: Offering multiple payment options such as credit/debit card, cash, and mobile payments can attract a wider range of customers and improve sales.

Look for a system that offers customer support: A system that offers customer support can provide assistance with setup and troubleshooting, which can help to minimize disruptions to your business.

Evaluate the cost of the system and additional costs: The cost of the system, including any additional costs such as transaction fees or monthly fees, should be evaluated to ensure that it fits within your budget.

Plan for implementation and training: Plan for implementation and training to ensure that your staff is familiar with the new system and able to assist customers with payments and troubleshoot any issues that may arise.

In conclusion, mobile payment and POS systems can provide convenience and efficiency for customers and business owners alike. By choosing a cloud-based system with inventory management and accounting software integrations, a built-in customer database, real-time reporting and analytics, a mobile app, multiple payment options, customer support and evaluating the cost, food truck business owners can find the best system for their business, streamline their operations, gain valuable insights into sales and customer behavior and improve the customer experience.

Another important consideration when choosing a mobile payment and POS system for your food truck business is the ability to accept mobile payments. Mobile payments such as Apple Pay, Google Wallet, and Samsung Pay are becoming increasingly popular among consumers, and accepting these forms of payment can help to attract customers and increase sales.

Additionally, consider a system that offers inventory management and tracking features. This will allow you to easily track your inventory and forecast for future needs. This can help you to manage your inventory more efficiently, reduce waste, and ensure that you always have the ingredients you need on hand to prepare your menu items.

Another consideration is the ability to track and analyze customer data. Many mobile payment and POS systems offer customer relationship management (CRM) features that allow you to store customer information and purchase history. This information can be used to create targeted marketing campaigns and improve customer loyalty.

When choosing a mobile payment and POS system, it is also important to consider the level of security provided. Look for systems that have built-in security features such as encryption, fraud detection, and data backup. This will help to protect your customers' personal and financial information, as well as your own business data.

Finally, it is essential to have a plan in place for training your staff on the new system. This will ensure that they are able to assist customers with payments and troubleshoot any issues that may arise. It's also important to provide ongoing training and support to ensure that your staff stays up-to-date with any new features or updates to the system.

In conclusion, there are many factors to consider when choosing and implementing a mobile payment and POS system for your food truck business. By considering factors such as mobile payments, inventory management, customer data tracking, security, and staff training, food truck business owners can find the best system for their business, streamline their operations, and provide a convenient and secure experience for their customers.

Food Truck Accounting and Bookkeeping: How to manage accounting and bookkeeping for your food truck business

Managing the accounting and bookkeeping for a food truck business can be a challenging task, but it is an essential aspect of running a successful business. Here are some strategies for managing accounting and bookkeeping for your food truck business:

Understand your financial statements: It's important to understand the financial statements of your business, including the balance sheet, income statement, and cash flow statement. These statements will provide a snapshot of your business's financial health and help you make informed decisions.

Create a budget: Create a budget for your business that includes projected income and expenses. This will help you to identify areas where you can reduce costs and increase revenue.

Keep accurate records: Keep accurate records of all financial transactions, including income, expenses, and inventory. This will help you to track your financial performance and identify areas for improvement.

Use accounting software: Use accounting software to manage your business's finances. This will help you to automate tasks such as invoicing, tracking expenses, and generating financial reports.

Track your inventory: Track your inventory to ensure that you have enough stock on hand to meet customer demand. This will help you to avoid stockouts and lost sales.

Understand your tax obligations: Understand your tax obligations and ensure that you are in compliance with all relevant laws and regulations.

Separate personal and business finances: Keep your personal and business finances separate to avoid confusion and ensure that you have a clear picture of your business's financial health.

Seek professional advice: Seek professional advice from an accountant or bookkeeper to ensure that your financial records are accurate and in compliance with laws and regulations.

Automate your bookkeeping: Automate your bookkeeping by using tools such as cloud-based accounting software, mobile apps, and receipt scanners. This will help you to stay organized, reduce errors, and save time.

Review your financial performance regularly: Review your financial performance regularly to identify areas for improvement and make adjustments as needed.

In conclusion, managing the accounting and bookkeeping for a food truck business is an essential aspect of running a successful business. By understanding financial statements, creating a budget, keeping accurate records, using accounting software, tracking inventory, understanding tax obligations, separating personal and business finances, seeking professional advice, automating bookkeeping, and reviewing financial performance regularly, food truck business owners can ensure that their finances are in order, understand their business's financial health, and make informed decisions to improve their business.

Another important aspect of managing accounting and bookkeeping for your food truck business is to have a clear understanding of your cash flow. Cash flow refers to the movement of money in and out of your business, and it is crucial to ensure that you have enough cash on hand to cover your expenses and pay your bills. One way to improve cash flow is to manage your accounts payable and receivable effectively. This means making sure that you are paying your bills on time and collecting payment from your customers in a timely manner.

Another way to improve cash flow is to manage your inventory effectively. By keeping track of your inventory levels, you can ensure that you are not overstocking on items that are not selling, and that you have enough stock on hand to meet customer demand. This will help to reduce waste and improve your bottom line.

Another important aspect of food truck accounting and bookkeeping is to manage your expenses effectively. This means keeping track of all of your expenses, including labor costs, food costs, and other operational expenses. By understanding your expenses, you can identify areas where you can reduce costs and improve your bottom line.

Finally, it is important to stay up-to-date with the latest tax laws and regulations. The tax laws and regulations for food truck businesses can be complex, and it is important to seek professional advice from an accountant or tax professional to ensure that you are in compliance with all relevant laws and regulations.

In conclusion, managing accounting and bookkeeping for a food truck business is crucial for the success of the business. By understanding financial statements, creating a budget, keeping accurate records, using accounting software, tracking inventory, understanding tax obligations, separating personal and business finances, seeking professional advice, automating bookkeeping, and reviewing financial performance regularly, food truck business owners can ensure that their finances are in order, understand their business's financial health, and make informed decisions to improve their business. Additionally, managing cash flow, inventory and expenses effectively, staying up-to-date with tax laws and regulations and seek professional advice can help the food truck business owners to improve their bottom line.

Inventory Management: How to manage inventory and track food cost effectively

Inventory management is a critical aspect of running a successful food truck business. It involves keeping track of the ingredients and supplies needed to prepare your menu items and ensuring that you have enough on hand to meet customer demand. Here are some strategies for managing inventory and tracking food cost effectively:

Create an inventory list: Create an inventory list of all the ingredients and supplies needed to prepare your menu items. This will serve as a reference when ordering and tracking inventory.

Track inventory levels: Track inventory levels to ensure that you have enough on hand to meet customer demand. This can be done manually or through the use of inventory management software.

Order inventory in a timely manner: Order inventory in a timely manner to avoid stockouts and lost sales. This will ensure that you have enough on hand to meet customer demand and that you are not overstocking items that are not selling.

Track food cost: Track food cost by keeping track of the cost of ingredients and supplies used to prepare each menu item. This will help you to identify areas where you can reduce costs and improve profitability.

Monitor food waste: Monitor food waste to ensure that you are not overproducing or throwing away food. This will help you to reduce costs and improve profitability.

Use a first-in, first-out (FIFO) system: Use a first-in, first-out (FIFO) system to ensure that the oldest inventory is used first. This will help you to reduce waste and improve the quality of your food.

Use technology to automate inventory management: Use technology to automate inventory management, such as cloud-based inventory management software, barcode scanning, and mobile apps. This will help you to stay organized, reduce errors, and save time.

Implement regular inventory counts: Implement regular inventory counts to ensure that your inventory levels are accurate and that you are not overstocking or understocking items.

Analyze your inventory data: Analyze your inventory data to identify trends and make adjustments as needed. This will help you to reduce costs and improve profitability.

Communicate with your suppliers: Communicate with your suppliers to ensure that you are getting the best prices on ingredients and supplies. This will help you to reduce costs and improve profitability.

In conclusion, managing inventory effectively is essential for the success of a food truck business. By creating an inventory list, tracking inventory levels, ordering inventory in a timely manner, tracking food cost, monitoring food waste, using a first-in, first-out system, automating inventory management, implementing regular inventory counts, analyzing inventory data and communicating with suppliers, food truck business owners can ensure that they have enough stock on hand to meet customer demand, reduce waste, and improve profitability.

Another important aspect of inventory management is to have a clear understanding of your food cost percentages. Food cost percentage is the percentage of the total sales revenue that is spent on food and beverage purchases. This percentage should be closely monitored, as it can have a significant impact on the overall profitability of your business. A food cost percentage that is too high can indicate that your menu prices are too low or that you are overspending on ingredients. On the other hand, a food cost percentage that is too low can indicate that you are overcharging for your menu items or that you are not using all of the ingredients you have purchased.

To calculate your food cost percentage, take the total cost of your food and beverage purchases and divide it by the total sales revenue for the same period. For example, if your total food and beverage purchases were $10,000 and your total sales revenue was $20,000, your food cost percentage would be 50%.

Another way to track your food cost percentage is by using a recipe cost calculator. This tool allows you to enter the cost of each ingredient used in a recipe, and it will calculate the cost per serving, as well as the cost percentage. This can be helpful for identifying recipes that are too expensive to produce and adjusting them accordingly.

Another key aspect of inventory management is to have good forecasting techniques. This means being able to predict future demand based on historical data and current trends. This will help you to plan your inventory purchases more effectively and reduce the risk of stockouts or overstocking.

Finally, it is important to have a system in place to handle inventory discrepancies. This means having a process in place to investigate and resolve any discrepancies between the physical inventory and the recorded inventory. This will help to maintain the accuracy of your inventory records and reduce the risk of inventory shrinkage.

In conclusion, inventory management is a critical aspect of running a successful food truck business. By creating an inventory list, tracking inventory levels, ordering inventory in a timely manner, tracking food cost, monitoring food waste, using a first-in, first-out system, automating inventory management, implementing regular inventory counts, analyzing inventory data, communicating with suppliers, monitoring food cost percentage, using recipe cost calculator and implementing forecasting and discrepancy management techniques, food truck business owners can ensure that they have enough stock on hand to meet customer demand, reduce waste, improve profitability and maintain accurate inventory records.

Food Truck Licensing and Certification: How to obtain the necessary licenses and certifications to operate your food truck business

Obtaining the necessary licenses and certifications is an important step in starting and operating a food truck business. These licenses and certifications ensure that your business is in compliance with local, state, and federal laws and regulations, and that your food is safe for consumption. Here are some key steps to obtain the necessary licenses and certifications for your food truck business:

Register your business: Register your business with your state's business registration office. This will typically involve obtaining a business license, tax ID number, and registering for sales tax.

Obtain a food service permit: Obtain a food service permit from your local health department. This permit will allow you to operate your food truck and serve food to the public.

Obtain a food handler's card: Obtain a food handler's card from your local health department. This card certifies that you and your staff have been trained in food safety and sanitation.

Obtain a mobile food vendor permit: Obtain a mobile food vendor permit from your city or county. This permit will allow you to operate your food truck in specific locations.

Obtain a commercial vehicle permit: Obtain a commercial vehicle permit from your state's department of motor vehicles. This permit will allow you to operate your food truck on the road.

Obtain a fire suppression system certification: Obtain a fire suppression system certification from a certified inspector. This certification ensures that your food truck's fire suppression system is in proper working order.

Obtain a food safety certification: Obtain a food safety certification from a recognized food safety organization. This certification ensures that your food truck meets food safety standards.

Obtain a liability insurance: Obtain a liability insurance to protect your food truck business from any lawsuits.

Comply with local zoning laws: Comply with local zoning laws to ensure that you are operating your food truck in the designated area.

Keep all licenses and certifications current: Keep all licenses and certifications current by renewing them as needed.

It is important to note that laws and regulations for food truck businesses can vary depending on the state and local government. Therefore, it is important to check with your local and state government for specific requirements and regulations that apply to your food truck business.

In conclusion, obtaining the necessary licenses and certifications is an important step in starting and operating a food truck business. By registering your business, obtaining a food service permit, obtaining a food handler's card, obtaining a mobile food vendor permit, obtaining a commercial vehicle permit, obtaining a fire suppression system certification, obtaining a food safety certification, obtaining a liability insurance, complying with local zoning laws, and keeping all licenses and certifications current, food truck business owners can ensure that their business is in compliance with the law and that their food is safe for consumption. Additionally, it is important to check with your local and state government for specific requirements and regulations that apply to your food truck business.

Another important aspect of obtaining licenses and certifications for your food truck business is to familiarize yourself with the health department regulations and requirements. These regulations and requirements can vary depending on the state and county, but they will typically include guidelines for food storage, preparation, and handling.

In addition to the health department regulations and requirements, it's also important to familiarize yourself with the specific codes and laws that pertain to food trucks. This includes regulations for parking, vending, and traffic. These laws can be different for each city and county, so it's important to research the specific laws in your area.

It's also essential to have all the necessary equipment and facilities to meet the health department regulations. This includes having a properly equipped kitchen, a handwashing sink, and refrigeration units to store food at the correct temperatures. Additionally, it's important to have a plan in place for handling food waste, as well as any other waste generated by your food truck business.

Another important aspect of obtaining licenses and certifications for your food truck business is to maintain accurate and up-to-date records. This includes keeping records of food safety and sanitation practices, inventory, and financial transactions. This will help you to stay organized, reduce errors, and save time.

In addition to the above-mentioned steps, it's also a good idea to join professional associations and networks, such as the National Food Truck Association or local food truck associations. These associations and networks can provide valuable resources, information, and support as you navigate the process of obtaining licenses and certifications.

In conclusion, obtaining the necessary licenses and certifications is an important step in starting and operating a food truck business. By familiarizing yourself with the health department regulations and requirements, researching specific codes and laws that pertain to food trucks, having all the necessary equipment and facilities, maintaining accurate and up-to-date records, and joining professional associations and networks, food truck business owners can ensure that their business is in compliance with the law and that their food is safe for consumption. Additionally, it is important to check with your local and state government for specific requirements and regulations that apply to your food truck business.

Another important aspect of obtaining licenses and certifications for your food truck business is to have a food safety plan in place. This plan should include procedures for preventing foodborne illness, such as proper food storage and handling, employee health and hygiene, and regular cleaning and sanitation of the food truck. This plan should be regularly reviewed and updated as necessary.

It is also important to have regular health inspections by the local health department. These inspections are usually required by law and are an important way to ensure that your food truck is operating in compliance with local and state regulations. The inspector will check for compliance with food safety regulations and will also check that all licenses and certifications are current and up-to-date.

It is also important to have a plan in place for dealing with food-borne illness outbreaks. This plan should include procedures for identifying and isolating affected food products, notifying the health department and other relevant authorities, and taking appropriate action to prevent further spread of the illness.

Another important aspect of obtaining licenses and certifications for your food truck business is to have a solid understanding of food labeling laws. The Food and Drug Administration (FDA) has specific laws that regulate what information must be included on food labels, such as ingredient lists, nutrition information, and allergen warnings. It is important to understand these laws and ensure that all food labels comply with them.

In conclusion, obtaining the necessary licenses and certifications is an important step in starting and operating a food truck business. By having a food safety plan in place, having regular health inspections, having a plan in place for dealing with food-borne illness outbreaks, having a solid understanding of food labeling laws and other health department regulations and requirements, researching specific codes and laws that pertain to food trucks, having all the necessary equipment and facilities, maintaining accurate and up-to-date records, and joining professional associations and networks, food truck business owners can ensure that their business is in compliance with the law and that their food is safe for consumption. Additionally, it is important to check with your local and state government for specific requirements and regulations that apply to your food truck business.

Handling Food Allergies and Special Dietary Needs: How to accommodate customers with food allergies and special dietary needs

Handling food allergies and special dietary needs is an important aspect of running a food truck business. Not only is it important to ensure the safety of all customers, but it can also help to attract a wider customer base and increase customer loyalty. Here are some key steps to accommodate customers with food allergies and special dietary needs:

Educate yourself and your staff: Learn about common food allergies and special dietary needs, such as gluten-free, vegan, and kosher. Understand the risks and symptoms associated with these conditions and how to identify them.

Have a clear labeling system: Use clear and specific labeling for all menu items, including allergen information. This can be done through the use of symbols or special labeling.

Offer a variety of options: Offer a variety of options for customers with food allergies and special dietary needs. This can include gluten-free, vegan, and kosher options.

Use separate equipment and utensils: Use separate equipment and utensils for preparing and handling allergen-free and special dietary needs food.

Train your staff: Train your staff to understand the importance of food allergies and special dietary needs and how to safely handle these foods.

Keep accurate records: Keep accurate records of allergen-free and special dietary needs foods. This will help to prevent cross-contamination and ensure that all customers receive the correct food.

Be prepared to answer questions: Be prepared to answer questions from customers about food allergies and special dietary needs.

Be willing to make adjustments: Be willing to make adjustments to menu items for customers with food allergies and special dietary needs.

It is important to note that food allergies can be life-threatening, so it's essential to take them seriously. By educating yourself and your staff, using clear labeling, offering a variety of options, using separate equipment and utensils, training your staff, keeping accurate records, being prepared to answer questions, and being willing to make adjustments, food truck business owners can ensure that they are able to accommodate customers with food allergies and special dietary needs safely and effectively. Additionally, it is important to check with your local and state government for specific requirements and regulations that apply to your food truck business.

In conclusion, handling food allergies and special dietary needs is an important aspect of running a food truck business. By educating yourself and your staff, using clear labeling, offering a variety of options, using separate equipment and utensils, training your staff, keeping accurate records, being prepared to answer questions, and being willing to make adjustments, food truck business owners can ensure that they are able to accommodate customers with food allergies and special dietary needs safely and effectively. Additionally, it is important to check with your local and state government for specific requirements and regulations that apply to your food truck business.

When accommodating with customers with food allergies and special dietary needs, it's essential to be transparent and upfront with them. This includes providing detailed ingredient lists, clear labeling on the menu, and ensuring that staff are trained to answer any questions customers may have.

It's also important to have a system in place for handling food allergies and special dietary needs. This can include using separate equipment and utensils for allergen-free foods, keeping accurate records of allergen-free and special dietary needs foods, and having a designated allergen-free preparation area in the food truck.

Another important aspect of accommodating with customers with food allergies and special dietary needs is to have a good communication with the customers. This can include having a clear and visible signage on the food truck, or having a dedicated section on the menu for allergen-free and special dietary needs options. This will help customers with food allergies and special dietary needs to easily identify options that are safe for them.

It's also important to have a flexible menu that can accommodate different dietary needs. This can include offering gluten-free, dairy-free, vegan, and kosher options. Offering a variety of options will help to attract a wider customer base, and increase customer loyalty.

In addition to the above steps, it's also a good idea to stay updated with the latest guidelines and regulations related to food allergies and special dietary needs. This can include subscribing to newsletters, attending industry conferences and events, and joining food truck associations and networks. These resources can provide valuable information and support as you navigate the process of accommodating with customers with food allergies and special dietary needs.

In conclusion, handling food allergies and special dietary needs is an important aspect of running a food truck business. By being transparent and upfront with customers, having a system in place for handling food allergies and special dietary needs, having good communication with the customers, having a flexible menu, and staying updated with the latest guidelines and regulations, food truck business owners can ensure that they are able to accommodate customers with food allergies and special dietary needs safely and effectively. Additionally, it is important to check with your local and state government for specific requirements and regulations that apply to your food truck business.

Managing Food Truck Employee Schedules: How to manage employee schedules and ensure adequate staffing

Managing employee schedules is an important aspect of running a successful food truck business. Having the right number of employees on hand at the right times can help to ensure that customers are served quickly and efficiently, while also reducing labor costs. Here are some key steps to managing food truck employee schedules:

Determine staffing needs: Determine the number of employees needed for each shift based on the volume of customers and the complexity of the menu.

Create a schedule template: Create a schedule template that can be used to plan employee schedules in advance. This template should include the shift start and end times, the number of employees needed for each shift, and the tasks that need to be completed during each shift.

Communicate the schedule: Communicate the schedule to employees well in advance, so they can plan accordingly. This can be done through email, text message, or an employee scheduling app.

Allow for flexibility: Allow employees to request schedule changes, such as swapping shifts or taking time off. This can help to ensure that employees are satisfied and motivated to work.

Monitor schedule adherence: Monitor schedule adherence to ensure that employees are arriving on time and staying for the duration of their shift.

Be prepared for unexpected absences: Be prepared for unexpected absences by having a list of employees who can cover a shift at short notice.

Train employees: Train employees on the food truck's policies and procedures, including schedules, to ensure that they are aware of their responsibilities and expectations.

Have a system for timekeeping: Have a system for timekeeping, such as a punch clock or an employee scheduling app, to ensure that employees are being paid for the hours they work.

Continuously evaluate: Continuously evaluate the schedule and make adjustments as needed to ensure adequate staffing and to improve efficiency.

In conclusion, managing employee schedules is an important aspect of running a food truck business. By determining staffing needs, creating a schedule template, communicating the schedule, allowing for flexibility, monitoring schedule adherence, being prepared for unexpected absences, training employees, having a system for timekeeping, and continuously evaluating the schedule, food truck business owners can ensure that they have adequate staffing and that employees are satisfied and motivated to work. Additionally, it is important to check with your local and state government for specific requirements and regulations that apply to your food truck business.

In addition to the above steps, it's also important to consider the following when managing food truck employee schedules:

Employee availability: Take into account the availability of each employee when creating the schedule. This can help to ensure that employees are able to work when they are available and that they are not overworked.

Overtime: Be mindful of overtime, as it can be costly for the business and may lead to burnout among employees. Consider ways to manage overtime, such as by hiring part-time employees or by scheduling breaks throughout the day.

Breaks and meal periods: Be sure to schedule breaks and meal periods for employees as required by law and company policy. This can help to ensure that employees are well-rested and able to perform their duties effectively.

Schedule and shift rotations: Consider rotating schedules and shifts among employees to promote fairness and prevent burnout. This can also help to keep employees motivated and engaged.

Employee preferences: Consider employee preferences when creating the schedule. For example, if an employee has a long commute, try to schedule them for shifts that are closer to their home to minimize travel time.

Communication with employees: Establish open communication with employees and encourage them to provide feedback on their schedules. This can help to identify any issues and make adjustments as needed.

Performance evaluations: Use performance evaluations to identify areas of improvement and to evaluate employees' ability to handle different schedules.

Future planning: Keep in mind future events, such as holidays, festivals and special occasions, when planning employee schedules. This will ensure that you are prepared to handle the increase in demand and have enough staff to handle it.

In conclusion, managing employee schedules is an important aspect of running a food truck business. By considering employee availability, overtime, breaks and meal periods, schedule and shift rotations, employee preferences, communication with employees, performance evaluations, and future planning in addition to the steps mentioned earlier, food truck business owners can ensure that they have adequate staffing and that employees are satisfied and motivated to work. It's important to stay updated with the latest laws and regulations related to employee scheduling and ensure that you are in compliance with them.

Food Truck Catering: How to expand your business by offering catering services for events and parties

Expanding your food truck business by offering catering services for events and parties can be a great way to increase revenue and reach new customers. Here are some key steps to take when offering food truck catering services:

Create a catering menu: Create a catering menu that is different from your regular menu and is tailored to the needs of the event or party. This can include larger portions, special dishes, and a variety of options to accommodate different dietary needs.

Establish pricing: Establish pricing for your catering services, taking into account the cost of ingredients, labor, and overhead.

Invest in catering equipment: Invest in catering equipment, such as chafing dishes, warming trays, and portable serving stations, to ensure that you can effectively serve and keep food at the right temperature during events.

Build a portfolio of previous events: Build a portfolio of previous events you've catered and use it to showcase your experience and the quality of your food.

Market your catering services: Market your catering services to potential clients through social media, your website, and by networking with other businesses and event planners.

Build relationships with venues: Build relationships with venues, such as hotels, banquet halls, and outdoor event spaces, as they may have a need for catering services for events they host.

Make sure your food truck meet health and safety regulations: Make sure your food truck meets all health and safety regulations, and that you have all necessary permits and licenses.

Be prepared for the event: Be prepared for the event by having a checklist of everything you need to bring, including food, utensils, and serving equipment, as well as a plan for setup, service, and cleanup.

Follow up with clients: Follow up with clients after the event to get feedback and testimonials, which can be used to promote your catering services in the future.

Continuously improve: Continuously improve your catering services by seeking feedback from clients, experimenting with new dishes and menus, and keeping up to date with industry trends.

In conclusion, offering catering services for events and parties can be a great way to expand your food truck business. By creating a catering menu, establishing pricing, investing in catering equipment, building a portfolio of previous events, marketing your catering services, building relationships with venues, making sure your food truck meet health and safety regulations, being prepared for the event, following up with clients, and continuously improving your catering services, food truck business owners can increase revenue and reach new customers. Additionally, it is important to check with your local and state government for specific requirements and regulations that apply to your food truck business catering service.

In addition to the steps mentioned above, here are some other considerations to keep in mind when offering food truck catering services:

Staffing: Make sure you have enough staff to handle the demands of catering events and parties. This may include additional staff for setup, service, and cleanup.

Transportation: Consider the logistics of transporting food, equipment and staff to the event location. Make sure you have the necessary vehicles, equipment and tools to transport everything safely and efficiently.

Kitchen Space: Make sure you have adequate kitchen space to prepare and cook food for catering events and parties. This may include renting kitchen space or renting a commercial kitchen.

Event Planning: Consider offering event planning services to clients, such as coordinating with other vendors, arranging rentals and decor, and handling other logistics.

Special requests: Be prepared to accommodate special requests, such as dietary restrictions or allergies. Make sure you have a clear understanding of the client's needs and that you have the necessary ingredients and equipment on hand.

Insurance: Make sure you have the necessary insurance to cover your food truck, equipment and staff during catering events and parties. This may include general liability, workers' compensation, and commercial auto insurance.

Contracts: Have written contracts in place for catering events and parties that outline the terms of service, including pricing, services provided, and any additional costs.

Payment: Establish clear payment terms with clients, including deposit and final payment due dates.

Permits and licenses: Make sure you have the necessary permits and licenses to operate your food truck at the event location and to serve food to the public.

Continuously evaluate: Continuously evaluate your catering services and make adjustments as needed to improve efficiency and customer satisfaction.

In conclusion, offering food truck catering services can be a great way to expand your food truck business. By keeping in mind staffing, transportation, kitchen space, event planning, special requests, insurance, contracts, payment, permits and licenses, and continuously evaluating your services, you can ensure that you provide a high-quality service and meet the needs of your clients. It's important to stay updated with the latest laws and regulations related to food truck catering and ensure that you are in compliance with them. Additionally, don't hesitate to reach out to your local Small Business Association or Chamber of Commerce for support and guidance.

Food Truck Expansion and Franchising: How to expand your food truck business by opening additional trucks or franchising

Expanding your food truck business by opening additional trucks or franchising can be a great way to increase revenue and reach new customers. However, it also comes with its own set of challenges and considerations. Here are some key steps to take when expanding your food truck business through additional trucks or franchising:

Assess your business: Assess your current business to determine if it is ready for expansion. Consider factors such as profitability, cash flow, and scalability.

Develop a plan: Develop a plan for expansion that includes details such as the number of additional trucks or franchises you plan to open, the location(s) of the new units, and the timeline for expansion.

Obtain financing: Obtain financing to fund the expansion. This may include loans from banks or investors, or crowdfunding.

Develop a brand: Develop a strong brand and image for your food truck business that can be easily replicated across multiple units. This will help to ensure consistency and recognition among customers.

Train staff: Train staff to ensure that they are equipped to handle the demands of running multiple trucks or franchises. This may include training on your business model, customer service, and food safety.

Create a standard operating procedure: Create a standard operating procedure (SOP) that outlines the processes and procedures for running your business. This will help to ensure consistency across all units.

Establish a support system: Establish a support system to provide assistance to franchisees or additional truck owners. This may include providing ongoing training, marketing support, and access to a network of other food truck business owners.

Legal considerations: Be aware of legal considerations when expanding your food truck business through additional trucks or franchising. This may include registering trademarks and patents, and complying with federal, state and local laws.

Continuously evaluate: Continuously evaluate the performance of your additional trucks or franchises and make adjustments as needed to improve efficiency and customer satisfaction.

Consider franchising: Consider franchising as an option to expand your food truck business. Franchising allows you to expand your business by allowing other entrepreneurs to use your brand and business model in exchange for a franchise fee.

In conclusion, expanding your food truck business through additional trucks or franchising can be a great way to increase revenue and reach new customers. By assessing your business, developing a plan, obtaining financing, developing a brand, training staff, creating a standard operating procedure, establishing a support system, being aware of legal considerations and continuously evaluating the performance of your additional trucks or franchises, you can ensure that your expansion is successful. Additionally, franchising is another option for food truck business owners looking to expand. It's important to stay updated with the latest laws and regulations related to food truck expansion and franchising and ensure that you are in compliance with them. Consult with legal and financial experts before making any decisions.

Conclusion: A summary of the key takeaways from the book and advice for starting a successful food truck business.

In conclusion, starting a food truck business can be a great way to enter the food industry and be your own boss. However, it also comes with its own set of challenges and considerations. The key takeaways from this book include:

Concept development: It's important to come up with a unique concept and menu for your food truck business that stands out in the market.

Business Planning: Creating a comprehensive business plan and determining your target market are crucial steps in starting a successful food truck business.

Financing: Securing funding and managing finances are important aspects of starting a food truck business.

Legal and Regulatory Requirements: Navigating the legal and regulatory requirements can be complex, but it is crucial to ensure compliance with all local and state regulations.

Vehicle and Equipment: Choosing the right vehicle and equipment is important to ensure the success of your food truck business.

Operations and Logistics: Plan for and execute the daily operations and logistics of your food truck business effectively.

Marketing and Promotion: Effectively market and promote your food truck business to reach new customers.

Managing Your Staff: Building a positive work culture and effectively managing your staff are important for the success of your food truck business.

Food Safety and Sanitation: Ensuring food safety and sanitation is crucial for the success and longevity of your food truck business.

Overcoming Challenges: Being prepared to overcome common challenges that food truck business owners face is crucial for long-term success.

Scaling and Growth: Growing and scaling your food truck business for long-term success requires a well-thought-out plan and strategies.

Location and Permits: Finding the right location and obtaining the necessary permits are important steps in starting a food truck business.

Insurance: Obtaining the necessary insurance to protect your food truck business is crucial.

Social Media and Online Presence: Building a strong online presence and effectively using social media can help you to reach new customers and promote your business.

Customer Service: Providing excellent customer service is crucial to attract and retain customers.

Menu and Food Cost: Developing a profitable menu and managing food cost effectively are important for the success of your food truck business.

Food Truck Design and Branding: Designing and branding your food truck to stand out in the market is crucial for success.

Food Truck Festivals and Events: Participating in food truck festivals and events can increase visibility and generate revenue.

Food Truck Associations and Networks: Joining food truck associations and networks can connect you with other food truck business owners and provide valuable resources.

Food Truck Safety and Maintenance: Maintaining your vehicle and equipment to ensure safety and longevity is important for the success of your food truck business.

Mobile Payment and Point of Sale Systems: Choosing and implementing mobile payment and point of sale systems can help streamline operations and improve customer service.

Food Truck Accounting and Bookkeeping: Managing accounting and bookkeeping effectively is crucial for the success of your food truck business.

Inventory

Management: Managing inventory and tracking food cost effectively can help to ensure profitability and minimize waste.

Food Truck Licensing and Certification: Obtaining the necessary licenses and certifications is crucial to ensure compliance and operate your food truck business legally.

Handling Food Allergies and Special Dietary Needs: Accommodating customers with food allergies and special dietary needs can help to increase customer satisfaction and attract a wider range of customers.

Managing Food Truck Employee Schedules: Managing employee schedules and ensuring adequate staffing is important to ensure smooth operations and great customer service.

Food Truck Catering: Offering catering services for events and parties can be a great way to expand your business and reach new customers.

Food Truck Expansion and Franchising: Expanding your food truck business through additional trucks or franchising can be a great way to increase revenue and reach new customers.

Conclusion: Starting a food truck business can be a great way to enter the food industry and be your own boss. However, it also comes with its own set of challenges and considerations. By following the advice and key takeaways from this book, you can increase your chances of starting a successful food truck business.

Advice for starting a successful food truck business includes: doing your research, developing a solid business plan, securing funding and managing finances effectively, ensuring compliance with legal and regulatory requirements, choosing the right vehicle and equipment, effectively planning and executing operations and logistics, marketing and promoting your business, effectively managing staff and ensuring food safety and sanitation, being prepared to overcome challenges, scaling and growing your business, and staying connected with other food truck business owners through associations and networks. It's also important to continuously evaluate your business and make adjustments as needed to improve efficiency and customer satisfaction. Additionally, stay updated with the latest laws and regulations related to food truck business and ensure that you are in compliance with them. Consult with legal and financial experts before making any decisions.